THE LAND IS ALWAYS ALIVE
The story of the Central Land Council

Central Land Council

ISBN 0 646 19364 3
© 1994 Central Land Council

This book is copyright. Apart from any fair dealing for the purposes of private study, research, criticism or review, as permitted under the Copyright Act, no part may be reproduced by any process without permission. Please forward any enquiries to the Central Land Council at the address below:

Central Land Council
PO Box 3321
Alice Springs NT 0871
Australia
Phone 089-516211
Fax 089-534343

Compiled by Peter McEvoy and Pamela Lyon
Designed by Christine Bruderlin
Map by Brenda Thornley
Cover Photograph by Mike Gillam

Thanks to D. Alexander, Neil Andrews, the Australian Institute for Aboriginal and Torres Strait Islander Studies, D. Avery, *Canberra Times*, Kunmanara Breaden, Shirley Brown, Angela Brennan, Di Calder, Chris Cope, Claire Colyer, Cecelia Dempsey, Geoff Eames, Mike Gillam, Lorrie Graham, Frank Hardy, Ross Howie, Institute for Aboriginal Development, Annie Keely, Jane Lloyd, Rosemary Murphy, D. Nash, Graeme Neate, Amy O'Donoghue, Wayne Pash, Bruce Petty, Michael Pickering, Richard Preece, Jonathon Rodd, D. Ross, Wenten Rubuntja, Toly Sawenko, Keith Smith, *Tennant & District Times, Centralian Advocate*, Andrea Watkins.

All photographs are the property of the Central Land Council unless otherwise stated. Every effort has been made to find the copyright holder of photographs and the Central Land Council would like to hear from anyone who has information regarding copyright of photographs.

Cartoons are reproduced with the kind permisssion of Bruce Petty and Michael Pickering.

The quote from Vincent Lingiari on page 7 was transcribed by Patrick McConvell and published in Luise Hercus and Peter Sutton (eds), *This is What Happened: Historical Narratives by Aborigines,* Australian Institute of Aboriginal Studies, Canberra, 1986, pp. 313–15.

Printed by Australian Print Group.

When European law was changed in 1976 so that we could win back control of some parts of our land many people thought that was the end of the story. They thought that we had won our fight.

But fifteen years later we are still fighting hard to win back control of our land and our sacred sites: fighting not just to go forward, but fighting against those people who want to push us back.

Every fight that we take up and every success that we win has come to us through years of struggle, and those years add up to the lives of Aboriginal people who are fighting to protect their land and their culture.

Mr Long Pwerle, CLC Chairman 1988–92

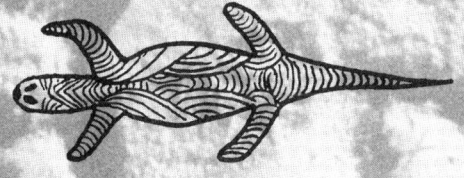

Contents

Foreword vii
We just want our land back 1
1974 5
   The Luritja Land Association 6
1975 7
   The CLC Region 8
1976 10
   The Land Rights Bill 13
1977 15
   Land Council Responsibilities 15
1978 17
   Warlpiri Land Claim 18
1979 20
   Willowra Land Claim 22
1980 23
1981 26
   Alice Springs Dam Part 1:
   Werlatye Atherre 27
   Defending the Land Rights Act 29
   Mt Barkly 30
   Lake Nash 32
1982 34
   Women 34
   Barrett Drive 35
   Little Well 37
1983 38
   Seven Years On 39
   Restructuring the CLC 41
   Land Management 42
1984 44
   Pushed Off Our Country 44
   Railway 47
   Office Space 48
1985 51
   Warumungu 52
   National Land Rights 56
   Uluṟu Handback 58

1986 59
   Pope John Paul's Visit 62
1987 63
   1987 Amendments 65
   We all belong to the songs 67
1988 69
   1988 March 70
   Barunga 73
   Mt Allan 77
1989 78
   Sacred Sites Protection 80
   The Yambah Mob 83
1990 87
   Barrow Creek Warriors 88
   Alice Springs Dam Part 2:
   Junction Waterhole 90
   Sacred Objects 94
1991 97
   Cubadgee 101
   Gurindgi 25 Years 103
   Kings Canyon Lodge 104
   For prime ministers to see,
   understand and honour 106
1992 107
   Mr Long Pwerle 110
   The Power Dispute 112
   McLaren Creek 115
1993 118
Glossary 126
Index 130

Foreword

Aboriginal spirituality, culture and society can be defined in one word: land. Land Councils give Aboriginal people a powerful and independent voice in the issues of their land – that is, their culture, their spirituality. When the history of Aboriginal land rights in Australia is finally written, the establishment of the Land Councils of the Northern Territory will be counted among the most important developments in that struggle.

Perhaps it is because Aboriginal people insist on setting their own priorities in relation to land and resist outside interference that the Land Councils have been maligned by government officials and the media and misunderstood by the public generally. This book has been published to help people understand what the Central Land Council is, and what it actually does.

For almost 200 years, government officials, missionaries and pastoralists made most of the decisions about where and how Aboriginal people lived. When Aborigines spoke about their love for the land and their responsibility to it, few listened. Even as more and more non-Aboriginal Australians became aware of the injustices done to Aboriginal peoples by colonisation and accepted the need to return some part of their land, government officials assumed that they, and not the Aboriginal landowners, would control the process of handing back the country.

This approach was turned about when in 1973 the newly elected Labor government appointed Justice Woodward to head a Royal Commission into Aboriginal land rights. This commission was to look at not whether, but how, land rights should be granted. Justice Woodward recognised that Aboriginal peoples needed to be independent of government in land matters, and one of the first things he recommended was the formation of both a central and northern land council in the Northern Territory to represent the views of traditional landowners.

The Department of Aboriginal Affairs organised the first formal meetings of the Central Land Council (CLC) in 1974, but Aboriginal people took over almost immediately, making it clear that Aboriginal people wanted to control their own affairs in this crucial area. They transformed the CLC into an independent Aboriginal organisation controlled by delegates representing communities throughout the region.

The legal recognition of Aboriginal land rights changed the lives of Aboriginal people in the Northern Territory. People who were once supervised by 'the Welfare' or 'the Mission' were now able to take control of their own communities and their own lives. Those who were rounded up and shifted to authorised settlements were able to return to their own country, to set up their own outstations and care for their land and sacred places.

Aboriginal people in Central Australia have accomplished a great deal through their representative Land Council and continue to do so, despite continuing strong opposition.

In the CLC region traditional landowners have won back 347,000 square kilometres of land. About half of that area was handed back after successful land claims, with the rest made up of former reserves and missions.

Traditional landowners have control over who enters their land and what they do there. However, contrary to the views of their adversaries, traditional landowners are keen to share their country and to develop their resources.

Each year the CLC issues more than 3,000 permits to tourists, mining companies, researchers and others seeking to enter Aboriginal land. As well, a wide range of commercial activities, including cattle operations, tourism ventures and mineral exploration and extraction, currently take place on Aboriginal land.

More than 10 per cent of the CLC region is now being mined or explored under agreements between the traditional landowners, mining companies and other developers for activities on Aboriginal land. Such agreements, of which there are more than two dozen, would not have occurred without the assistance of the CLC. Oil, gas and gold are all extracted from Aboriginal land in Central Australia for the benefit of all Australians. The traditional landowners share in these benefits through royalties and negotiated payments. This money is used for community development projects and investment in Aboriginal enterprises as well as individual payments to traditional landowners.

Aboriginal people are striving to achieve lasting economic security through their own enterprises. With the assistance of the CLC, they are establishing cattle companies and tourist ventures; they are setting in place sound land management practices, and developing community infrastructure, such as water supplies, shelter, power, roads and so forth, for existing communities and remote outstations.

The CLC has also helped Aboriginal people set up an enterprise/development agency, secure productive investments in major tourist ventures such as Kings Canyon Wilderness Lodge and Central Australia's largest motor vehicle dealership, establish an airline which serves remote communities and to develop the Tanami Network – a widely acclaimed two-way video conferencing system that links remote communities to each other and to agencies and corporations across the world.

Yet, even with these achievements, the hard struggle to gain justice for Aboriginal people and improve the conditions of their lives continues. It is a distressing fact that living conditions on many Aboriginal communities in the Northern Territory sink below Third World standards. In a recent study, it was revealed that 13,000 Aboriginal people live in communities without reticulated water. The struggle to improve these conditions and provide education, training and employment opportunities has never been greater.

Looking back over the history of the CLC the most frustrating battles have been to defend Aboriginal rights from groups with vested interests in their land. Such groups would rather work against Aboriginal people than with them. These recurring campaigns, often led by the Northern Territory Government, have attempted to weaken the Land Rights Act, to obstruct land claims and to promote divisions in the Aboriginal community.

The fight to obtain even small living areas for Aboriginal people whose land was taken for cattle operations and other developments before the Land Rights Act has been long and frustrating. The battle to protect sacred sites has often been openly antagonistic and at times insulting to Aboriginal people.

By their words and deeds, government officials frequently give the public the impression that the Land Councils have too much power and manipulate or impose their views on Aboriginal people. But the Land Councils are only an instrument of traditional landowners' will.

The CLC is a council of Aboriginal people representing their own communities. They make the decisions on everything from excisions policy to mining agreements. The CLC's involvement in issues such as protection of sacred sites and the defence of the rights established under the Land Rights Act is a direct result of traditional landowners' profound concerns. Attacks on the so-called power of the Land Councils are really attacks on the limited power of the Aboriginal peoples they represent.

There is no question that Aboriginal peoples have come a long way since the passage of the Land Rights Act. But there is still a long way to go. The job of holding on to what little has been won does not get any easier, and that makes it more important than ever to remember our history so that we can continue to move ahead.

This book brings together the story of the Central Land Council for the first time. The people who made these stories are the thousands of Aboriginal people who have kept their culture and language alive and maintained their land and their law. They have been assisted by CLC staff – administration workers, anthropologists, field staff, land management specialists, lawyers and many others. They have all worked together to bridge the gap between Aboriginal and non-Aboriginal people and cultures.

CLC is proud of its achievements and recognises that most of the stories told here barely scratch the surface of the effort and struggle which went into the making of them. But the goal is constant and can be largely summed up in the words of Wenten Rubuntja, a long-time CLC member and former Chairman: 'That's the Land Rights Act: your law and my law is standing as one. Two different, different laws standing as one.'

Kumantjayi Ross

We just want our land back

In 1963 the people of Yirrkala Mission in Arnhem Land submitted a petition – a traditional bark painting – to the Commonwealth Parliament. They asked for recognition of their rights as the traditional owners of their land.

The Yirrkala people challenged the Commonwealth Government's legal power to issue a mining lease at Gove without the consent of traditional landowners. It was not the first time that Aboriginal people had challenged their dispossession, but it was the first time in 180 years that they had been able to make their challenge in the Australian courts.

Eight years later, in April 1971, their claim was rejected. The Northern Territory Supreme Court ruled that the traditional landowners' property system was not recognised under Australian law and that Australia was terra nullius, an empty land, prior to 1788.

It was not until the Mabo decision, in the early 1990s, that the fiction of terra nullius was finally overturned; but the intervening decades represented the most significant years in the history of land rights for Aboriginal people.

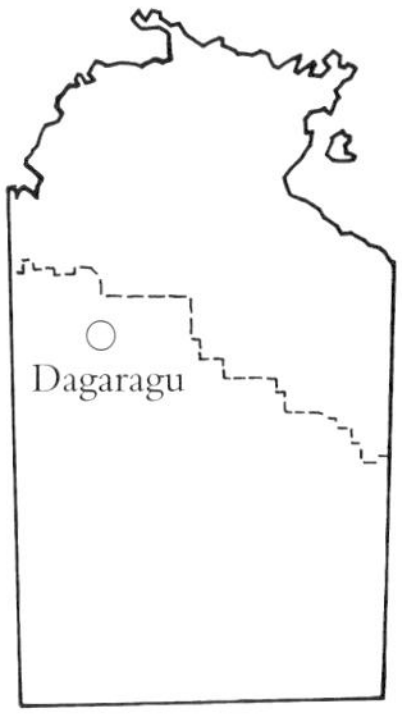

On 22 August 1966 the Gurindji people, working as stockmen and station hands in the north-west of Central Australia, walked off Wave Hill Station, then owned by England's Lord Vestey. Soon after, they set up permanent camp on part of their traditional land, at Daguragu, a waterhole on Wattie Creek. At first this was seen to be no more than a 'blackfella's' strike for wages and better working conditions. In fact it was the start of the political struggle that led to the Aboriginal Land Rights Act and the story of the Central Land Council.

Until this time, Aboriginal labour had been the cornerstone of the pastoral industry in Central Australia, but Aboriginal men and women received only a meagre share of the wealth they created. Zero wages and miserable living conditions for Aboriginal workers were common and strikes had occurred in the Pilbara in the 1940s and later at Newcastle Waters and Brunette Downs. In the 1960s it was still common for skilled Aboriginal workers to be paid nothing more than a little tobacco, tea, flour and sugar.

Billy Bunter Jampijinpa is one of those who took part in the walkoff and who remembers the old days:

We were treated just like dogs. We lived in humpies. You had to crawl in and out on your knees. There was no running water. The food was bad – just flour, tea, sugar and bits of beef – like the head or feet of a bullock.
Victor's father [Vincent Lingiari] came back from hospital in Darwin and he had decided that he would pull us out. He pulled everyone out that Tuesday and we walked with the kids and our swags to the Victoria River where we camped until Christmas.

The Vestey's mob came and said they would get two killers [slaughtered cattle] and raise our wages if we came back. But old Victor's father said, 'No, we're stopping here'. Then in 1967 we walked to our new promised land. We call it Daguragu. Back to our sacred places and our country, our new homeland.

In March 1966 the Arbitration Commission ruled that Aboriginal pastoral workers should be paid equal wages. The court's decision was to be phased in over three years.

But the Gurindji people were not seeking wages. They were fighting to win back their land and refused to return to work even when Lord Vestey offered to pay some 'money' wages. Gurindji leader Vincent Lingiari told Lord Vestey, 'You can keep your gold. We just want our land back.'

In April 1967, with the help of author, the late Frank Hardy, they petitioned the Governor-General, Lord Casey, for the return of part of their tribal land, including Daguragu. Their petition was rejected by Lord Casey, who warned them against breaking the law and interfering with the rights of the pastoral lessee.

The Gurindji maintained their position. They resisted the threats, harassment and cajoling of pastoralists, politicians and public servants and put land rights on the national political agenda, speaking at public meetings 'down South' and building support from Aboriginal and non-Aboriginal people and organisations throughout Australia.

Mick Rangiari recalls the protest years:

I went down a couple of times. First year I went for three months, second year I went for six months.
Even young boys and girls in the University – I went down to give them a speech. Even little ones in that public school.
Some of the young ones in the University used to come into my house and they tell me about it: 'Make us really sad you know that story. It's not good. Not in Australia. It's your land! They should give you a fair go.'
Vestey didn't want us to tell everyone but we talked plenty.
A lot of change been coming afterwards. I been doing a lot of talking.
I've seen a lot of change. We live together now. And we from bad way we live good way now. You know – a lot of people getting land. Very important.
I think it's better now today. We talk about it and we're the people that make the decision. Central Land Council do a lot of work. Fixing up the land. Everybody seems to work together. Aboriginal people and Kardiya [non-Aboriginal people]. They all work together now. When I been a karu [a child] we didn't even talk to white people.
Mick Rangiari, Gurindji leader

National interest in their case increased, attracting attention not only to their struggle for land but also to the appalling conditions under which so many Aboriginal people lived. The late Fred Hollows, an eye surgeon, was inspired by a talk given in 1968 by Vincent Lingiari about the walkoff. He later went to Wattie Creek to examine people's eyes in the Gurindji camp. What he saw there sparked his involvement in the first Aboriginal medical service in Redfern and in a national program to fight trachoma and other eye diseases in remote communities:

It was a shock to me. I'd been working at the hospital and in my private practice and seeing a parade of eye disorders, but nothing like this... It was like something out of the medical history books – eye diseases of a kind and degree that hadn't been seen in western society for generations! The neglect this implied, the suffering and wasted quality of human life were appalling.

Meanwhile, the Federal Council for the Advancement of Aborigines and Torres Strait Islanders (FCAATSI) successfully campaigned for a referendum to give the Commonwealth Government the power to make laws relating to Aboriginal people. On 27 May 1967 Australian voters overwhelmingly supported the 'full citizenship' referendum with a record 89 per cent 'yes' vote.

FCAATSI and other groups hoped the victory would spur quick and positive action to improve the lives of Aboriginal people.

After the referendum the Commonwealth Government established an Office of Aboriginal Affairs but there was still no progress on land rights.

At that time the Commonwealth Government was a coalition of two conservative parties: the Liberals who were based in the cities and the Country Party which represented rural conservatives. The Country Party was strongly opposed to any recognition of Aboriginal peoples' rights to their traditional land, and so despite growing national support for the Gurindji and sympathetic statements from some Liberal Party members, the Government refused to recognise the justice of the Gurindji's claim.

Peter Nixon, the Minister for the Interior, summed up the Country Party view in September 1970: 'It is wholly wrong to encourage Aboriginals to think that because their ancestors have had a long association with a particular piece of land, Aboriginals of the present day have the right to demand ownership of it.'

But the Gurindji and their supporters continued to press their case and the national campaign for land rights continued to build.

In February 1972 Aboriginal protesters set up an Aboriginal Tent Embassy on the lawn outside Parliament House in Canberra. The Embassy highlighted the dispossession of Aboriginal people and attracted national and international media attention and public support. However, the Government remained intransigent and in July that year ordered police to forcibly remove the Embassy.

The recognition of land rights was now Labor Party policy and opposition leader, Gough Whitlam, visited the Tent Embassy to personally express his support for the protest.

We will legislate to give Aborigines land rights – not just because their case is beyond argument, but because all of us Australians are diminished while the Aborigines are denied their rightful place in this nation.
Gough Whitlam, ALP Policy Speech, November 1972

It was an opportune statement of support. In the federal election of December 1972, the Liberal–Country Party Government, after twenty-three years in office, was defeated by Labor. In keeping with their promise, the new government moved quickly on the issue of land rights, and appointed Justice Woodward to head a Royal Commission into how land rights should be implemented in the Northern Territory.

The Labor Government wound up the old Welfare Branch of the Department of the Interior which had actively opposed the Gurindji, and transferred its responsibilities to the new Department of Aboriginal Affairs in 1973. In July that year a Commonwealth parliamentary committee called for protection of traditional Aboriginal rights at Uluru (Ayers Rock) and recommended that traditional landowners be given a central role in management of the proposed national park.

At the same time Justice Woodward delivered his interim report recommending the establishment of central and northern land councils in the Northern Territory to represent traditional landowners.

He delivered his Second Report in April 1974, setting out procedures for Aboriginal land claims and conditions of land tenure, including control over mining. He recommended that Aboriginal people should be able to claim unalienated crown land, Aboriginal reserves and Aboriginal-owned pastoral leases where they were able to prove traditional affiliation, and make claims over small areas on pastoral properties and in towns on the basis of need. Justice Woodward recommended that the land councils should help lodge land claims, protect Aboriginal interests in land (including sacred sites) and assist Aboriginal land owners in the management and use of their land.

Today, twenty years after the CLC was formed, Aboriginal people are still struggling to have their land restored to them. From its beginnings in the 1960s, with the Yirrkala petition and the Gurindji walkoff, the story of contemporary land rights is one of determination against impossible odds. Many of the people who started the campaigns did not live long enough to see their land returned, but they are remembered in this history, and their land is always alive.

1974

JUNE

➤ In line with the recommendations of Justice Woodward, the Department of Aboriginal Affairs organises the first meeting of the Central Land Council.

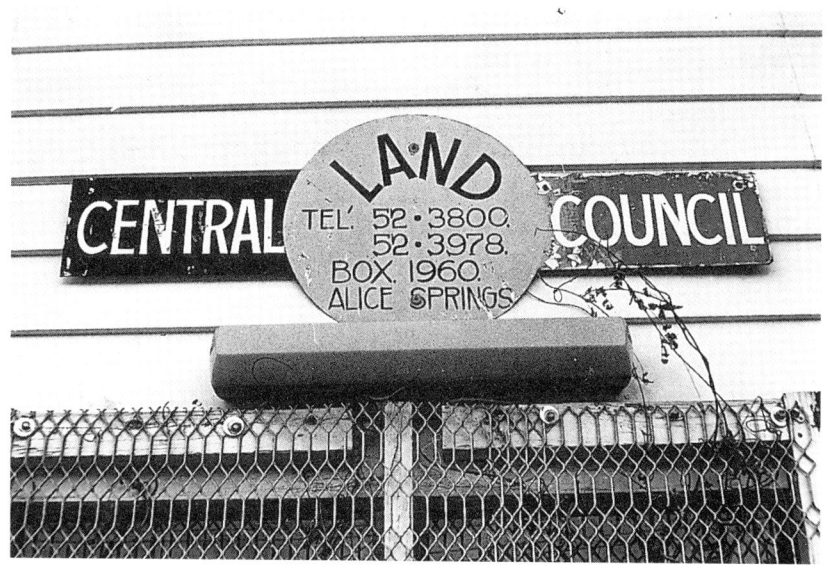

NOVEMBER

➤ The Aboriginal Land Fund Commission Bill is introduced. Since 1973 the Whitlam Government has allocated $5 million per year for land purchases throughout Australia, but the Department of Aboriginal Affairs (DAA) has been timid about spending the money. The Bill is passed in December and Martin Jampijinpa from Willowra, a property purchased by DAA in 1973, becomes a member of the Aboriginal Land Fund Commission

THE LURITJA LAND ASSOCIATION

In October 1974 a number of Luritja families, whose traditional land lies north-east of Uluru, formed the Luritja Land Association to press their claims for their country. They were particularly interested in land covered by two pastoral leases: Tempe Downs and Middleton Ponds.

Kunmanara Breaden first asked the Department of Aboriginal Affairs to buy Tempe Downs for the Luritja in 1973 and in the years that followed approaches were made to five different ministers for Aboriginal Affairs.

In the mid-70s Mr Breaden's family and another group led by Sid Coulthard moved onto Tempe Downs and Middleton Ponds without title despite the opposition and intimidation of pastoralists and managers.

In 1974 the families applied to lease an area south of Tempe Downs but were told that the land was 'unsuitable for any pastoral pursuits'. The area was at first part of the Ayers Rock (Uluru) land claim but later became part of the Lake Amadeus/Luritja land claim. After that claim was lodged the Northern Territory Government 'leased' the area to commercial operators, and although the lease was later declared invalid by the High Court, the Government's action led to long and complicated legal actions which are still preventing the area from being returned to the traditional landowners.

In 1983 part of Tempe Downs was acquired by the Northern Territory Government to create Kings Canyon National Park. Kings Canyon, which the Luritja call Watarrka, is a part of an area of great significance to the traditional landowners and they argued strongly that they should own the land and jointly manage the Park. Instead the traditional landowners were only given an advisory role by the Government.

In 1983 Ben Clyne, one of the founding members of the Luritja Land Association, summed up the frustration that he and others felt:

> *For ten years we've been asking quietly, 'Can we have some land? here? here? or where?' And all the time it's the same. They say, 'No you can't have it'. This time we're told it's for tourists. Before it was for cattle. All the time it's the same.*
>
> *What is more important, human beings or birds? Might be Aboriginal people are more important, or is it birds and lizards?*
>
> *We're not against tourists, not trying to stop them, but they just come and go away again. We want to go and stop there, to look after our country forever.*

After twenty years of quietly asking, the Luritja people finally won their fight. In December 1993 they purchased Tempe Downs and Middleton Ponds with ATSIC funding and lodged a land claim to secure their title to the land.

1975

➤The second Central Land Council meeting is held at Amoonguna, east of Alice Springs. The meeting considers how traditional landowners should be represented.

FEBRUARY 28–29

➤The Central Land Council meets at Amoonguna. The two-day meeting is attended by eighty delegates representing forty-seven communities. DAA staff summarise the recommendations of Woodward's Second Report and the Council resolves to hold regional meetings to choose delegates to represent all language groups.

APRIL 3–4

➤Prime Minister Whitlam hands over the lease to Daguragu Station. This was 3,236 square kilometres of land purchased from Wave Hill Station by the Gurindji with money provided by the Aboriginal Land Fund. To symbolise the transfer Mr Whitlam pours a handful of soil into the hands of Vincent Lingiari, one of those who led the walkoff and held the community together through eight years of struggle.

AUGUST

Nyawa jangkakani katiya-ma ngaliwa-nguny ngumpit-ku mula-ngkura patati-yiri warik-kara ngu-lu yan-i nyampa-yala-ni kula nyampa-wu, kuya-wu-wala.
Ngu-laa ngali jimari kar-u katiya ngumpin nyawa karwa-lu langa-nka-ma kula welfare-kari-wu kula welfare-kari-wu.
Ngura ngu-ngala-ngkulu ka-nya, ngu-lu linkara ka-nya lurpu.

These important white men have come here to our ceremonial ground and they are welcome because they have not come for any other reason — just for this handover.
We will be mates – White and Black. You Gurindji must keep this land safe for yourselves. It does not belong to any different 'welfare' man.
They took our country away from us; now they have brought it back ceremonially.
Vincent Lingiari, 16 August 1975

➤Justice R.C. Ward, a judge of the Northern Territory Supreme Court, is appointed Interim Aboriginal Land Commissioner. The first case he hears in Central Australia is the Suplejack land claim. The claim is lodged by the Central Australian Aboriginal Legal Aid Service (CAALAS) on behalf of Warlpiri traditional landowners when a pastoralist tries to lease the area. In 1977 the traditional landowners withdrew their claim over most of Suplejack Station in a negotiated settlement during the Warlpiri and Kartangarurru–Kurintji land claim.

THE CLC REGION

The Central Land Council represents traditional landowners throughout the Central Australian region of the Northern Territory — an area of 780,000 square kilometres which includes more than twenty language groups. Aboriginal people living in major towns, town camps, remote communities, former reserves, national parks, outstations on Aboriginal land and excisions and stock routes on pastoral land are all represented. Reflecting the interests of this diverse group has always been a major priority for the CLC. The earliest meetings before the passing of the Aboriginal Land Rights Act focussed on the need to reflect the full range of different language and regional groups and the CLC has tried to strengthen its regional representation throughout its history.

The 1983 Coombs Report (see p.41) recommended a restructuring of the Council and Executive to ensure that all major regions are represented. The Central Land Council is made up of eight regions and each region elects a representative to the CLC Executive. Three other executive members — the Chairman, Deputy Chairman and one extra member — are elected from the whole of the Council.

The CLC has also established regional offices at Tennant Creek, Kalkarindji, Mutitjulu, Papunya and Atnwengerrp to improve the level of service available to traditional landowners who live a long way from the central office in Alice Springs.

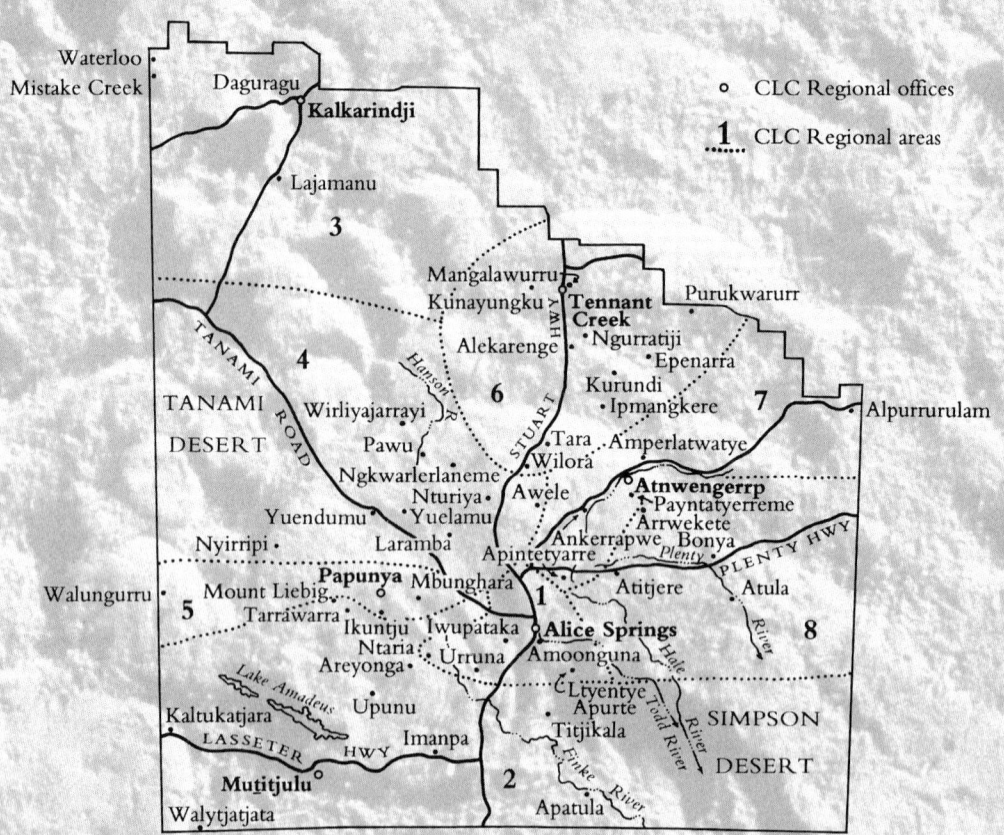

1975

➢ The budget allocation to the Aboriginal Land Fund Commission is cut back to $2 million because of Commonwealth Government financial problems.

SEPTEMBER 16–17

➢ The Central Land Council meets in the basement of the Elkira Court Motel in Alice Springs. The Aboriginal delegates make it clear that their council must be independent of the Department of Aboriginal Affairs, with its own office and staff.

Charles Perkins is elected as Chairman, Wenten Rubuntja is elected Vice Chairman and Geoff Eames is seconded from Central Australian Aboriginal Legal Aid Service (CAALAS) to be the first CLC lawyer.

The Council considers the proposed Aboriginal Land Bill, directs the staff to begin preparation for land claims, including needs-based claims in Alice Springs, and investigates the possibility of the Aboriginal Land Fund Commission purchasing pastoral leases.

OCTOBER

➢ The Whitlam Government introduces the Aboriginal Land (Northern Territory) Bill 1975 into Parliament. The Bill proposes land rights in the Northern Territory based on the Woodward recommendations with land claimed on grounds of need as well as traditional affiliation and traditional landowners maintaining control over mining and development.

NOVEMBER

➢ Justice Ward begins hearing the needs-based claim for Alice Springs town camps. The claim, which involves twelve sections of land, is organised by Wenten Rubuntja in two weeks of creekbed meetings with traditional landowners. Justice Ward states publicly that he is likely to recommend that all the land be granted, but the hearing is never finished.

➢ On 11 November 1975 the Governor-General, Sir John Kerr, dismisses Gough Whitlam and his Government. Parliament is dissolved before it can finish considering the Aboriginal Land (Northern Territory) Bill. Caretaker Prime Minister Malcolm Fraser orders Justice Ward to stop hearing land claims, and calls an election for 13 December.

In the Northern Territory the election campaign is bitterly fought. The Australian Mining Industry Council, pastoralists and the Northern Territory administration mount a massive media campaign against land rights. On the national scene the main issues are the economy and the dismissal and Whitlam is swept from office in a landslide victory for Malcolm Fraser and the Liberal–Country Party coalition.

1976

JANUARY ➤ During the election campaign the Liberal–Country Party promised 'no change' on land rights policy under a Fraser Government, but now they propose major amendments including the virtual abolition of the land councils. The CLC joins with other Aboriginal organisations to fight back and counter the pressure of the anti-land rights lobby.

MARCH 18 ➤ A thousand Aboriginal people march in Alice Springs for land rights and the Land Councils. The march knocks the wind out of Northern Territory administration claims that the Aboriginal people don't support land rights.

People travel hundreds of miles from Daguragu in the north-west and Ernabella in South Australia in a stunning demonstration of Aboriginal support. It is a turning point that makes non-Aboriginal people realise that the land rights issue is here to stay.

Following the march, an Aboriginal deputation led by Wenten Rubuntja campaigns for land rights across the country, culminating in a meeting with Prime Minister Fraser in Canberra. Mr Rubuntja carries a *tjuringa* (sacred object) to the meeting as a symbol of authority.

JUNE ➤ The Fraser Government introduces the Aboriginal Land Rights (Northern Territory) Bill into Parliament. The new Bill weakens the Land Councils, prevents claims over Aboriginal-owned pastoral leases and gives the Northern Territory Government responsibility for passing legislation for the protection of sacred sites and land claims based on need. The CLC

1976

In April 1976 the CLC published the first *Central Australian Land Rights News*. The roughly typed and copied newsletter pulled no punches:

> **CENTRAL AUSTRALIAN LAND RIGHTS NEWS**
>
> Have a look at our first edition. Terrible is'nt it? It may get better but don't hold your breath waiting.
>
> This is the year of land rights in the Northern Territory. Victories won now will establish the pattern for the next fifty years of development in Aboriginal Affairs. If you want the inside information on what Aborigines are doing to win Land Rights then the newsletter won't tell you. But it may give the odd hint.

Fifteen years later *Land Rights News* is jointly published by the Central and Northern Land Councils. With a circulation of over 20,000 it is distributed to every major Aboriginal community and to subscribers throughout the world.

strenuously objects to several sections of the Bill and negotiations continue through the rest of the year.

Meanwhile, mining companies approach CLC seeking to work on areas which are likely to become Aboriginal land. The CLC gathers expert advice and details of proposals for traditional landowners to consider fully.

A few days after the Bill is introduced Wenten Rubuntja is elected CLC Chairman at a council meeting at Amoonguna, east of Alice Springs. Aboriginal Affairs Minister Ian Viner attends the meeting and promises the Commonwealth will overrule any Northern Territory law which doesn't truly protect sacred sites.

When my father was alive — he's been finish up along Amoonguna with all them old fellas — they use to say 'We got to get our land back sometime, because our land got Law.'
Well that been come up news come about land rights and they said 'Yeah, we gotta get land rights now.' They come to a protest 'Land rights Now. Land rights Now.' That's all the way along.
Centre people didn't have nothing then. Arrernte people just lived anywhere: town, tents, humpies and all mixed up only.
We been thinking that land rights is a good thing. Good thing for work and good thing for live.
I like to talk about that one, because this government came over and asking questions of Aboriginal people about what we want. Well we got to ask them for land, if they going to give us land back, or you know,

1976

that we got to do. And how we going to work the country back. That's what we were thinking about inside.
If Europeans want to get land, they say how much? How many acres can you buy?
We've got to go back and ask our Aboriginal Law. Grandmother's and Grandfather's country — that's the country we've got to get.
We gotta find out from our culture country and you got to find out from your law. See? That's the Land Rights Act: your law and my law is standing as one. Two different, different laws standing as one.
Wenten Rubuntja, CLC Chairman

AUGUST ➢ The Finke River Mission joins the land rights debate. Pastor Paul Albrecht and Professor Ted Strehlow campaign against land rights and the Land Councils, and the Mission holds a series of bush meetings telling Aboriginal people that the CLC wants to control Aboriginal land and have power over who profits from mining royalties. They tell non-Aboriginal people that land rights and land councils are inconsistent with 'the Aboriginal reality' and launch a vicious and personal attack on CLC Chairman Wenten Rubuntja.

The campaign is finally discredited at a large meeting of Aboriginal people convened by the Mission in November. Geoff Eames speaks to the meeting and dispels misunderstandings about the role of the CLC. Pastor Albrecht loses support when he refuses to read the text of his own public statements to the gathering. Many Aboriginal people who had doubts about the CLC now become active members.

In retrospect, the debate with Finke River Mission was of great importance for the survival of the CLC. It taught the staff lessons about the need to maintain our grass roots contacts. It generated a debate on the legislation which certainly produced a real awareness of the terms of the legislation and provided a model for future processes of consultation.
Geoff Eames, CLC Lawyer 1975–78

➢ The Aboriginal Land Fund receives no funding in the Commonwealth budget.

DECEMBER ➢ The *Aboriginal Land Rights (Northern Territory) Act 1976* is passed. The Act has been amended but is still significantly weaker than Woodward's recommendation and the Whitlam Bill.

Under the Act, land which had been designated as Aboriginal reserve is converted to Aboriginal land without having to be claimed (so-called Schedule I land). In the CLC region these areas are Amoonguna, Finke River Mission (Hermannsburg), Haasts Bluff, Jay Creek, Hooker

THE LAND RIGHTS BILL

The Aboriginal Land Rights Bill introduced into Parliament by Aboriginal Affairs Minister Ian Viner in June 1976 was considerably weaker than the Bill proposed under Whitlam or the recommendations of Woodward. While miners, pastoralists and the Northern Territory Country Liberal Party pressured the Government to delay the Bill and water down land rights even more, the CLC joined other Aboriginal groups to push for a stronger law.

The Central Land Council met with Mr Viner and representatives from the Northern Territory Assembly at Amoonguna. The delegates were strongly opposed to plans to allow the Northern Territory administration to pass complementary legislation – particularly on sacred sites – and told Mr Viner straight out that they believed the CLP members were 'anti-Black'.

They were scathingly critical of local CLP member Roger Vale who attended the meeting with Mr Viner.

'Roger Vale do you understand the law about Aboriginal land? You talk the wrong way,' said Dick Leichleitner Japanangka from Yuelamu. 'We read the story in the paper. The land was the same when Captain Cook came. You are only a young man but you rubbish us all the time. You only fight for the station owners. You know —— all. You don't know the stories.'

At the meeting the Minister invited the CLC to send him a written submission on their concerns about the Bill and promised to carefully consider the criticisms of delegates. Of course the CLC wasn't the only group lobbying the Government which was besieged with submissions from both pro and anti-land rights groups. Defence Forces Ombudsman David Hay was appointed to consider all the submissions and when the Act was finally passed in December 1976 it contained forty-three amendments. The Land Councils' role in representing Aboriginal land interests is restored and Aboriginal landowners have the right to veto exploration and mining on their land, but the Northern Territory Government is still authorised to pass complementary legislation on sacred sites, entry by government employees onto Aboriginal land, and land claims based on need including town camps and pastoral excisions.

The two most important failures of the final Act were that it contained no provision to meet the land needs of Aboriginal people who have been dispossessed by pastoralists and towns, and no adequate protection for sacred sites. Despite the strong representation by the Land Councils, the Fraser Government decided to leave legislation in both areas up to the Northern Territory Government.

1976

Creek (Lajamanu), Lake Mackay, Petermann, Santa Teresa, Warrabri (Alekarenge) and Yuendumu.

Land Rights to me is a very good thing, one of the good things that I have seen. They shouldn't muck about too much, but they should give that land straight back. To the people who hold on in the Northern Territory, they should give tribal land and sacred sites back straight away instead of holding on to it. A place like Suplejack, we are waiting for, it is 'frozen' in Aboriginal and European law. Suplejack is one of the most sacred sites to our Warlpiri people and it seems right for us to get it back; but we don't say, 'Get out!' to those staying there; we say, 'Don't touch it; leave it alone'.
The late Maurice Jupurrula Luther MBE, Lajamanu 1976

1977

➢ The *Aboriginal Land Rights (Northern Territory) Act 1976* becomes law. John Toohey, a Western Australian QC, is appointed the first Aboriginal Land Commissioner in August.

JANUARY 26

The granting of land rights to Aboriginals recognises not only the justice of prior claims to ownership, it also recognises the validity of Aboriginal traditional law and cultural values…
It will provide for the Aboriginal people a land base for future social advancement according to their own cultural values and their own aspirations and importantly, in their own time. What we require now is the goodwill of the people of Australia to make this legislation work. White Australians are not unaware of their own attachment to the soil. To

LAND COUNCIL RESPONSIBILITIES

Although the CLC was already up and running in 1977, the passing of the Aboriginal Land Rights (Northern Territory) Act gave the Council new statutory powers and responsibilities, which are set out in section 23 of the Act:
- find out and express the opinions of Aboriginal people on the management of Aboriginal land in the CLC region;
- protect the interests of Aboriginal people in the Land Council area;
- assist Aboriginal people to take measures to protect sacred sites on all land in the Land Council area;
- consult traditional landowners about any proposal to use Aboriginal land (e.g. mineral exploration, mining, pastoral activity, tourism etc.);
- negotiate on behalf of traditional Aboriginal owners with people (e.g. mining companies, pastoralists, land developers etc.) who want to use Aboriginal land or land under claim;
- assist Aboriginal people in making land claims, particularly by arranging and paying for legal assistance for claimants;
- keep a register of Land Council members and members of Land Trusts (Aboriginal land-holding bodies) in the Land Council area; and
- provide administrative support and assistance for Aboriginal Land Trusts in the CLC area.

The CLC also has statutory responsibilities to:
- attempt to conciliate any dispute between Aboriginal people over land matters;
- hold in trust and distribute to Aboriginal associations payments from the Aboriginals Benefits Trust Account and income earned under negotiated agreements;
- process applications for permits to enter Aboriginal land; and
- assist Aboriginal people in native title claims and negotiations.

1977

Aboriginals it is more. It is their very life, the source not only of their spirit but of the place to which their spirit must return. They are indivisible with their land. It is life itself. It is the force that has enabled them to survive for 40,000 years. It has been the strength of their fight – now won – for their birthright.
Ian Viner, Minister for Aboriginal Affairs in the Fraser Government, at the proclamation of the Land Rights Act, 26 January 1977

FEBRUARY 3–4 ➢ The Minister for Aboriginal Affairs, Ian Viner, joins over 300 Aboriginal delegates from communities throughout Central Australia at the first meeting of the Central Land Council since its incorporation under the Land Rights Act. Wenten Rubuntja is re-elected as Chairman and Don Ferguson is elected as Deputy Chairman. The meeting chooses a full council of nearly seventy members to represent all the Aboriginal communities in the CLC region.

MAY ➢ The Commonwealth Government declares Uluru (Ayers Rock–Mt Olga) National Park, effectively transferring the ownership of the Park to the Director of the National Parks and Wildlife Service. The area had been reserved as a national park since 1958 but until this time had remained crown land. The declaration prevents traditional owners from claiming their land under the Land Rights Act.

1978

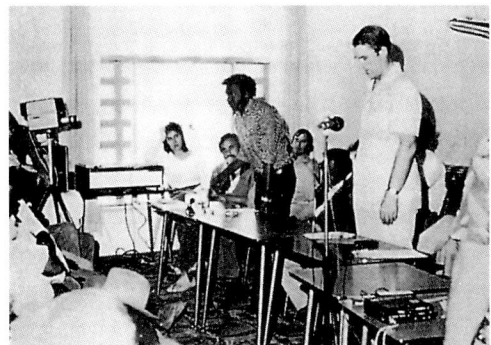

APRIL
➢Prime Minister Malcolm Fraser, Aboriginal Affairs Minister Ian Viner and the Country Liberal Party's Northern Territory Legislative Assembly leader, Paul Everingham, attend a CLC meeting in Alice Springs.

JUNE
➢The Northern Territory Government introduces 'complementary legislation' which, among other things, denies Aboriginal people the use of cattle station bores and requires non-Aboriginal approval for protection of sacred sites. The legislation fails to address the land needs of Aboriginal town campers or those living on pastoral properties.

➢The CLC organises negotiations between traditional landowners and Magellan Petroleum regarding oil and gas drilling at Mereenie Basin near Haasts Bluff, west of Alice Springs.

JULY
➢The Northern Territory is granted self-government. Paul Everingham, the leader of the Country Liberal Party, becomes the first Chief Minister and soon lifts the freeze on new leases of vacant crown land. The freeze was introduced by Prime Minister Whitlam in 1974 to allow breathing space for the Woodward Commission and the preparation of land claims. The move means that vacant crown land can be alienated by the Northern Territory Government and so become unavailable for claim under the Land Rights Act. The Chief Minister promises that he won't take any action that will interfere with land claims, and writes to the CLC: 'It is not the intention of the Northern Territory Government to attempt to avoid the intentions of the [Land Rights Act].' This promise is repeatedly broken.

AUGUST
➢Toohey recommends that the entire Warlpiri land claim – 95,000 square kilometres of land – be returned to traditional owners. People begin moving back to their traditional country but some are unable to return due to lack of essential services such as water.

SEPTEMBER
➢The Utopia land claim hearing is adjourned when Chief Minister Paul Everingham asks the High Court to prevent the claim going ahead. The Northern Territory Government argues that the claim should not be heard because the land is a pastoral lease and that the Aboriginal Land Fund Commission, which purchased the station, does not hold the

WARLPIRI LAND CLAIM

The Warlpiri and Kartangarurru–Kurintji land claim was the first land claim heard under the *Aboriginal Land Rights (Northern Territory) Act* in the CLC region.

The area under claim was largely desert country – fertile traditional land had been seized for cattle – but the claim was still strenuously opposed by the Northern Territory Government. The Territory Parks and Wildlife Commission argued that traditional landowners would shoot out rare species and destroy the ecology of the Tanami Desert Wildlife Sanctuary.

The traditional landowners reached amicable agreements with the lessees of Suplejack and Rabbit Flat Roadhouse but the Northern Territory Government opposed the claim to the bitter end.

After 3,000 pages of hearing transcript and 175 exhibits Land Commissioner Toohey recommended that the entire area under claim be handed back to the traditional landowners – a recommendation accepted by Aboriginal Affairs Minister Ian Viner.

'We're the first ones and we were born there,' Jerry Jangala explained during the land claim hearing. 'Not only myself but my big brother and my big sisters were born before that Wildlife [Sanctuary]. They were born there and they will grow up there. Even my father was born there, my mother was born there, my grandfather. They were there while Tanami Wildlife [Sanctuary] was coming and we're the ones, the first ones and I think they can ask us what they can do about their wildlife.'

Today traditional landowners co-operate with natural resource scientists, and assist in the conservation of endangered species.

1978

land 'on behalf of Aboriginal people'. This is the first of many attempts by the Northern Territory Government to use the courts to block claims. While almost entirely unsuccessful, these legal challenges delay and frustrate the land claim process and traditional landowners.

Mr Everingham we don't like what you are doing trying to stop our claim to make Utopia Aboriginal land. We hold the land in a stronger way than whitefellas. We hold it from our fathers and our grandfathers. We hold it as Kurtingurlu.
We can't leave our country behind. If we go away bad things will happen. Somebody might get killed if we go somewhere else. We can't leave this country. We have to hold this land. It has our dreamings and sacred places. We've got sacred everything here.
This has been our land, it has been our food, for a long long time, this country. You just can't hold us up again, like whitefellas did before.
A letter signed by 100 traditional landowners from Utopia

➤ The Tiwi Land Council is formed to represent the traditional landowners of Bathurst and Melville islands. These islands had been part of the Northern Land Council region but the Aboriginal Affairs Minister, Ian Viner, establishes a separate land council following representations from the Tiwi people for recognition of their distinct cultural and geographic identity.

➤ The Northern Territory Government amends the Crown Lands Ordinance to allow sub-leases for Aboriginal living areas, but at the same time pushes through amendments to restrict Aboriginal rights on pastoral properties. These changes weaken Aboriginal rights to enter, camp, hunt and collect bush foods on pastoral properties that have been recognised in non-Aboriginal legislation since pastoral leases were first granted in 1863.

NOVEMBER

➤ The Warumungu land claim (to areas of vacant crown land near Tennant Creek), the Warlmanpa land claim (to vacant crown land west of Tennant Creek towards Wave Hill) and the Willowra land claim (to the Aboriginal-owned Willowra pastoral lease) are lodged with the Aboriginal Land Commissioner.

1979

MAY ➤ The Northern Territory Government increases the size of Territory town boundaries to include large areas of land under claim. The move is an attempt to frustrate the claims – under the Aboriginal Land Rights Act areas inside town boundaries can't be claimed.

The town of Tennant Creek (population 3,100) suddenly covers 710 square kilometres — thirty times larger than the old boundaries. Darwin is made four times the size of Greater London and Katherine becomes the world's largest city! Later, the Alice Springs Town Council attempts to have that town's area expanded from sixty to 1,600 square kilometres. All these boundary changes are later declared invalid by the courts but they do succeed in delaying and frustrating claims through long and expensive legal actions.

JUNE ➤ The mining lobby and the Northern Territory Government campaign for amendments to the Land Rights Act to remove traditional landowners' control over access for exploration and mining. They claim that 'black tape' is tying up the land, but Aboriginal Affairs Minister Fred Chaney says the hold-up is caused by mining companies' unwillingness to negotiate: the companies have been encouraged by industry bodies and the Northern Territory Government to stall negotiations as a tactic in the push for amendments.

Mr Chaney says the Act will not be changed and that miners should get back to work. Magellan Petroleum, which has taken a leading role in the campaign, resumes its talks with CLC over the Mereenie Oil and Gas Field.

AUGUST ➤ The Governor-General, Sir Zelman Cowan, executes deeds of grant to Aboriginal land trusts for former Aboriginal reserve land at Amoonguna, Haasts Bluff, Hooker Creek (Lajamanu), Iwupataka, Lake Mackay, Petermann Reserve, Santa Teresa and Yuendumu. The Northern Territory Registrar-General refuses to register these deeds.

SEPTEMBER ➤ The *Aboriginal Sacred Sites Act 1979 (NT)* comes into effect, establishing the Aboriginal Sacred Sites Protection Authority (ASSPA). The CLC have continually argued that protection of sacred sites should be a Commonwealth responsibility and an earlier draft of the Bill was rejected by a Commonwealth parliamentary committee because it gave the Northern Territory minister control over the protection of sacred sites. In this version of the Act the ASSPA is controlled by Aboriginal people but its powers are limited and it does not ensure that new works are subject to a sacred sites clearance.

1979

OCTOBER

➤ The Northern Territory Government notifies the Gurindji traditional landowners that it intends to take back Daguragu Station.

In 1975 Prime Minister Whitlam told the Gurindji that the land would belong 'to you and your children forever', but the Northern Territory Government says it will be resumed in twenty-eight days because the traditional landowners have not kept to the pastoral lease conditions. The Gurindji prevent the resumption when they demonstrate that not only have lease conditions been met but the property is well managed.

To secure the title to their land the Gurindji lodge a land claim over the property.

➤ The Warlmanpa land claim hearing begins in Alice Springs and takes evidence at Alekarenge and in the Tennant Creek area.

NOVEMBER

➤ Aboriginal Affairs Minister Fred Chaney appoints Barry Rowland QC, the former Chairman of the Western Australian Law Reform Commission, to review the practical implementation of the Land Rights Act. The review is established in response to political pressure from the Northern Territory Government for changes to the Act, but the Government makes no submission to Mr Rowland.

WILLOWRA LAND CLAIM

The Willowra land claim is one of many in Central Australia that was delayed and obstructed through legal action by the Northern Territory Government. The station was purchased by the Department of Aboriginal Affairs in 1973 and held in trust for the Willowra community. In November 1978 the CLC lodged a land claim on behalf of the traditional landowners, but the hearing, which had been scheduled to begin in December 1979 was postponed because of the Northern Territory Government legal action over the Utopia land claim.

The late Jampijinpa Martin wrote to the Chief Minister on behalf of the Willowra.

The Willowra land claim should have started yesterday. We were ready. You have asked for it to be put off. That makes the people at Willowra very angry. Nobody is telling us what to do. We started ourselves pushing for land rights. We have been doing that for many years. The individual owners asked for that. Creed Lovegrove [Northern Territory Government official] knows. Everyone knows.

We have been promised that we could make a traditional land claim under the Land Rights Act. The Commonwealth Government promised that in the Australian Parliament. We don't forget that. That is the word of the Government. You say that you are going to fight our claim, to block it like Utopia. That is breaking the Commonwealth law about land rights. That is breaking the law, the word we have been given. That is really serious. It is very wrong. You should be keeping the promise. If you break the promise they should put you along to court.

We are running the place properly. We are looking after the cattle, selling them and paid all our debts. A lease for fifty years is not strong enough for us. This is our land, our tribal area, our fathers and grandfathers and uncles and mothers land.

We are one community here. All the Warlpiri people at Yuendumu, Mt Allan, Hooker Creek and Chilla Well support us. You should come and talk to the community. Don't send Les Penhall [Northern Territory Government official]. We want to talk to you.

The High Court delivered its judgement against the Northern Territory Government in February and the Willowra land claim began hearings in April 1980.

The area claimed covered the upper Lander River, where many of the Coniston Massacre killings took place. Jampijinpa of Willowra was just a small boy in 1928 but he remembers seeing his father shot by Constable Murray.

'Down at Tipinpa, That's this Murray bin shottit. When I was little fella.'
Were you there when they shot your father?
'Yeah. Little one. When I was little boy 'bout that high, I think. I seen him. I seen him. Murray, Murray grab me then and he's hold me on the shoulder. When I was little fella. That far, that's all I know that far.'*

Title to Willowra was handed back to traditional landowners in July 1983.

* *Long Time, Olden Time*, P & J Read, 1991, IAD Publications, p.45.

1980

FEBRUARY

➤ The High Court rejects a Northern Territory Government legal challenge and rules that the Utopia pastoral lease is available for claim. The decision also clears the way for hearings to commence on other pastoral leases under claim. This is the first of a long string of defeats for the Northern Territory Government in the Federal and High Courts in relation to land claims.

➤ The CLC and traditional landowners reach an agreement with Magellan Petroleum over the Mereenie Oil and Gas Field.

➤ The Northern Territory Government establishes an inquiry into pastoral land tenure. A committee chaired by Alice Springs solicitor (now Chief Justice) Brian Martin and including Surveyor General Peter Wells and NLC manager Wes Lanhupuy, will report on a number of matters including 'the needs of Aboriginals'.

MARCH

➤ A thirty-ton boulder is taken from Kunjarra — the 'Devils Pebbles' — and placed in a park in Tennant Creek. Kunjarra is a sacred site of great significance to the Warumungu people and the desecration is blamed for the death of a senior custodian. The Warumungu campaign for fifteen months until the boulder is eventually returned.

➤ The CLC lodges a land claim on behalf of Wakaya–Alyawarr traditional landowners for the Wakaya Desert, 200 kilometres east of Tennant Creek.

APRIL

➤ Former Prime Minister Gough Whitlam meets with the CLC in Alice Springs, and visits Yuendumu, Willowra, Utopia and Tennant Creek. At Yuendumu he is shown a display of more than thirty painted shields.

1980

MAY
➤ The Willowra land claim hearing begins. The hearing had been scheduled for December 1979 but was adjourned because of the Northern Territory Government's challenge to the Utopia land claim.

➤ The outstation or homelands movement is gaining momentum and more and more Pintupi move to Kintore (near the Western Australian border) from Papunya (a former government ration depot). About 150 Pintupi are living at Kintore at this time, but the community's only resources are a hand-pump bore, thirteen iron humpies, one shed used as a store and a two-way radio.

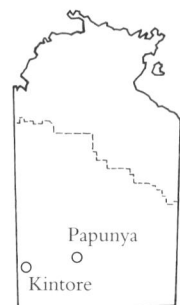

➤ After negotiations between the Land Councils, the Commonwealth Government and the Northern Territory Government, the Northern Territory Registrar General agrees to register the titles to the areas of former Aboriginal reserves which became Aboriginal land under the Land Rights Act. The Act is amended to ensure that public roads are maintained.

JUNE
➤ Aboriginal Land Commissioner John Toohey recommends that the whole of the Willowra land claim be granted to the traditional owners.

OCTOBER
➤ The Martin Committee delivers its report on pastoral land tenure in the Northern Territory. The recommendations are very disappointing for dispossessed traditional landowners since they rely on the agreement of pastoralists to establish any living area.

In the past the white man shot our people and took the country. They didn't ask. They set up cattle stations and used the black people to build the station up and make them rich. Now Aboriginal rights have come. The Northern Territory Government wants to refuse the right to claim freehold title to land and mining rights.
Land is important for Aboriginal people, to live there and have tribal customs and culture and sacred things. We are not trying to kick white people out. We can only buy stations when they are up for auction or sale. It is important for Aboriginal people to go back to their own country. If they have their own land they can stay away from trouble in towns. We give the cattlemen money for land. They never gave money to us. They just took it. We give them money and then we can try for Aboriginal title.
The late Jampijinpa Martin, CLC Delegate from Willowra

1980

NOVEMBER

➢ Mr Barry Rowland QC delivers his report on the practical operation of the Aboriginal Land Rights Act to the Commonwealth Government. After a year-long examination he recommends no major changes to the legislation.

DECEMBER

➢ The CLC meets in Alice Springs and elects Stanley Scrutton as Chairman. Kunmanara Breaden is elected Deputy Chairman, and outgoing Chairman Wenten Rubuntja remains on the CLC Executive and is employed as Special Adviser.

1981

➢ Four years after the Land Rights Act, more than forty areas of land are under claim in the CLC area, and fourteen areas have been handed back. The CLC is working in co-operation with the Department of Aboriginal Affairs and the Aboriginal Development Commission for excisions on eight stations: Mt Skinner, Lake Nash, Yambah, Hamilton Downs, Middleton Ponds, Maryvale, Napperby and Ambalindum.

➢ Negotiations begin with Magellan Petroleum on development of the Palm Valley Gas Field with a pipeline to Alice Springs, and with North Flinders Mines on development of a gold mine in the area of the Granites, north-west of Yuendumu. The CLC reaches an agreement with Pancontinental to ensure that sacred sites are protected in a seismic work program on Aboriginal and pastoral land.

FEBRUARY ➢ The Northern Territory Government's opposition to the basic principles of the Land Rights Act continues and Chief Minister Paul Everingham proposes a package of amendments to the Act. The package would stop claims over Aboriginal-owned stations, stock routes, stock reserves and national parks, and severely restrict the ability of Aboriginal people to apply for living areas on pastoral leases. A series of meetings is held with the Land Councils, the Northern Territory Government and the Commonwealth to resolve differences, but Mr Everingham's proposed amendments are not accepted by the Commonwealth.

The Federal Minister has got a problem too. They are pushing him from one side and we're pushing him from the other side. How should we get around pastoralists? We should try and talk to them and they should talk to us. Then we know the problem then we can see clear.
When we are talking to them, don't get hot and hot. Talk really smooth. If they talk that way and say 'you're not going to get your land', don't start making it hot straight away. Leave and come back and talk again.
The late Jampijinpa Martin of Willowra

➢ The Australian National Railways approaches CLC to ensure that a proposed railway line from Alice Springs to Darwin does not interfere with sacred sites. The CLC agrees to consult traditional landowners to identify an acceptable route as far as Elliot while the Aboriginal Sacred Sites Protection Authority is commissioned to clear the northern part of the corridor.

MARCH ➢ Traditional landowners, for the area around the Alice Springs Telegraph Station, meet to discuss the Northern Territory Government's plan for a recreation lake that would inundate and destroy important sacred sites,

ALICE SPRINGS DAM PART 1: WERLATYE ATHERRE

The traditional landowners of urban areas have to deal not only with the social and cultural impact of past dispossession but continuing pressure to expand and develop any remaining land with little regard for its cultural and sprititual significance.

In Alice Springs the process of dispossession continues and until recently traditional landowners lacked the legal protection and political strength to successfully resist development which would desecrate and destroy sacred sites, but traditional landowners' struggle to defend sacred sites in the Todd River has been a turning point. The fight to defend these sacred sites has covered more than a decade and has focussed on Northern Territory Government proposals to dam the Todd River for a recreation lake or flood mitigation dam.

A recreation lake was first proposed in 1979 and in March 1983 Northern Territory Chief Minister Paul Everingham announced construction near the Alice Springs Telegraph station would soon begin. The lake would destroy and desecrate a number of sacred sites including Werlatye Atherre, an important part of the Two-Women Dreaming which extends north and south of Alice Springs connecting different language groups throughout Central Australia. Traditional landowners had consistently told the Northern Territory Government that Werlatye Atherre, which was registered under the Northern Territory Government Sacred Sites Act, could not be destroyed, but Mr Everingham was determined to proceed.

A few weeks after the announcement the traditional landowners established a protest camp near the Alice Springs Telegraph Station. The camp was visited by Aboriginal Affairs Minister Clyde Holding who promised Commonwealth action to prevent the destruction of Werlatye Atherre. He proposed a joint Commonwealth–Northern Territory Government Tribunal to examine the lake proposal from all aspects. The traditional landowners maintained the protest camp for six months until a fire caused two tragic deaths and the protesters had to leave the camp area in accordance with Aboriginal tradition.

When the Tribunal delivered its report in August 1984 it found that the significance of Werlatye Atherre made the area unsuitable for any recreation lake.

The Northern Territory Government reluctantly dropped the proposal but in 1988 a large flood claimed the lives of three Aboriginal river-campers. Although the Telegraph Station proposal had been for a recreation lake not a flood mitigation dam, new Chief Minister Steve Hatton blamed the traditional owners of Werlatye Atherre for the deaths and the Northern Territory Government renewed its push.

Deputy Chief Minister Barry Coulter announced feasibility studies into the construction of a combined flood mitigation and recreation dam at the Telegraph Station in April 1988. A number of meetings were held over the next twelve months but the traditional landowners consistently rejected any proposal to damage or desecrate Werlatye Atherre and called on the Northern Territory Government to consider alternative flood mitigation.

1981

including Werlatye Atherre, a sacred site of great importance to women and part of the Two-Women Dreaming. The traditional landowners ask the CLC for help and send a letter to Chief Minister Paul Everingham stressing the importance of the sacred sites and the need to protect them. Mr Everingham announces that the Government will go ahead with the lake at the Telegraph Station anyway.

APRIL ➤ The Mary Ann Recreation Dam at Tennant Creek is officially opened by local MLA Ian Tuxworth. The dam reserve includes land that has been under claim since 1978 when the Warumungu land claim was first lodged. The dam was built without consulting the traditional landowners and will permanently submerge an important group of sacred sites.

MAY ➤ The Northern Territory Government purports to offer a lease for a substantial part of the Lake Amadeus/Luritja land claim area to Messrs Ian Conway and Tim Lander. The Government's action attempts to alienate the land and prevent the claim. The area affected is the same one that the Luritja families wanted to lease in 1975. They were told then that the land was dry and unsuitable.

The 'lease' is in breach of Everingham's commitment not to alienate land under claim and in 1988 the Federal High Court rules that the 'lease' was never valid.

➤ The Mt Barkly pastoral lease, 360 kilometres north-west of Alice Springs, is purchased by the traditional landowners using profits generated on the neighbouring Willowra pastoral lease. A land claim over Mt Barkly is lodged in June.

➤ Angarapa Aboriginal Land Trust receives title to Utopia, the first pastoral station successfully claimed by Aboriginal people.

AUGUST ➤ A Northern Territory Government-Department of Aboriginal Affairs working party proposes amending the Land Rights Act to deal with the

DEFENDING THE LAND RIGHTS ACT

The defence of land rights is a recurring theme in the history of the CLC. From the start powerful interest groups have opposed the Aboriginal Land Rights Act because the legal recognition of the rights of traditional landowners gives them control over access to their land. Governments, developers, miners and pastoralists can no longer simply push Aboriginal people off their land to build, or mine, or run their cattle, unfettered. They must recognise the rights of Aboriginal people and negotiate with them as equals. Some have refused to accept this new reality and more effort has often been put into trying to revoke the statutory rights of Aboriginal people than to working with them.

In February 1981 the Northern Territory Government made a written submission to the Commonwealth calling for a package of amendments to the Land Rights Act. The Northern Territory had made no submission to the twelve-month inquiry into the Act by Barry Rowland QC, who delivered his report in November 1980, but now they proposed major changes.

Aboriginal Affairs Minister Peter Baume arranged a series of meetings between the Land Councils, the Commonwealth and the Northern Territory Government.

The amendments proposed by the Northern Territory Government were extensive. They wanted an end to land claims over pastoral leases, areas under grazing licence, park reserves and stock routes, a deadline for land claims so that no new claims could be made after a certain date, and reduced Aboriginal control over exploration and mining. The Northern Territory Government threatened to 'go its own way' and the Commonwealth Government was unwilling to defend its own legislation, but the Land Councils refused to concede their rights.

In June 1982 the new Minister for Aboriginal Affairs, Ian Wilson, and Chief Minister Paul Everingham jointly announced amendments to prevent land claims over Aboriginal-owned pastoral leases, stock routes, reserves and national parks. The amendments became known as the Ten-Point Package and provided for perpetual lease title for excisions, Aboriginal pastoral leases and some national parks including Uluru. Mr Everingham backed up the package with an address to the National Press Club and a $200,000 advertising campaign. The Central, Northern and Tiwi Land Councils joined with the Pitjantjatjara Council to stage a more modest campaign: they published one press advertisement and distributed a small booklet which rebutted the Chief Minister's arguments. CLC Chairman Stan Scrutton, Executive Member Geoff Shaw and Yami Lester from the Institute for Aboriginal Development travelled to Sydney, Melbourne and Adelaide to speak to the media.

The Ten-Point Package was dropped when the Hawke Labor Government was elected in March 1983. The new Commonwealth Government came to power with a policy for strong national land rights but the pressure and momentum of the anti-land rights lobby was building.

1981

question of living areas and stock route claims. The amendments would prevent Aboriginal people who have been forced off stations from applying for living areas, give the Northern Territory Minister for Lands the final say on applications and not provide secure title. Mr Everingham says that this is the Northern Territory Government's last word, but the proposals are unacceptable to the CLC.

OCTOBER ➤ The *Pitjantjatjara Land Rights Act 1981* (SA) is proclaimed after a five-year struggle by the Pitjantjatjara, Yankunytjatjara and Ngaanyatjarra people. Their traditional country straddles the borders of the Northern Territory, South Australia and Western Australia. The South Australian legislation provides 103,000 square kilometres of land in that state under inalienable Aboriginal freehold title, complementing the Aboriginal land,

MT BARKLY

Mt Barkly was the first pastoral lease in the Northern Territory to be purchased directly by Aboriginal people.

The station, which is 360 kilometres north-west of Alice Springs, was purchased in 1981 using profits from the neighbouring Willowra Station, which is also Aboriginal owned.

Mt Barkly has only marginal viability as a cattle property but covers areas and sites of great significance to the people at Mt Barkly and Willowra and neighbouring communities at Alekarenge, Anningie, Lajamanu, Mt Allan, Ti-Tree and Yuendumu.

The traditional landowners lodged a land claim to the station in November that year and the claim was heard in June 1983. Claimant Rosie Nungarrayi described how she and her family fled Mt Barkly to escape killings at Willowra in the late 1920s.

> We were living at Wirliyajarrayi when the troublesome whiteman Nugget Morton was living at Mud Hut. He shot people in those days. Frightened by him we travelled camouflaged in the scrub bush, drinking from soakages only at night when it was darker and cooler. We drank from the soakage at Pawu [Mt Barkly] and continued on to Ngarnka [Mt Leichhardt], still frightened.
> My relations were murdered by this whiteman, finished by him.
> We dug for yarla [bush yams] and gathered yakajirri [currants], wanakiji [bush tomato], yawakiyi [bush plum] and marningkiji [conkerberry].

Title to the land was handed back to the traditional landowners in December 1986.

1981

and land under claim in the Northern Territory. The traditional owners still have no land rights in Western Australia.

More and more Anangu came, and Anangu's power grew like a battery being charged up. And when people went to meetings and meetings and talked and talked we got the land back. We got our land back so we can look after all the sacred sites properly and look after other beautiful things on our lands in the same way that a long time ago our people kept them beautifully.
Punch Thompson, Chairman of Pitjantjatjara Council 1981

NOVEMBER

➤ The Mereenie Oil and Gas Field agreement between CLC and Magellan Petroleum is signed. The agreement was actually finalised in February 1980 but the formal signing was delayed for almost two years because of a dispute between the Northern Territory Government and Magellan.

DECEMBER

➤ The Northern Territory Aboriginal Heritage Bill is introduced into the Legislative Assembly. The new Bill would compromise the power of Aboriginal custodians to define their own sites and put matters of Aboriginal Law under the direction of the Northern Territory Minister for Lands. The proposed law is strongly opposed by the CLC and other Aboriginal organisations and is never passed.

➤ The Kaytej (Kaytetye), Warlpiri and Warlmanpa land claim hearing begins before Justice Toohey, taking evidence at Alekarenge and Alice Springs over the next two months.

The hearing revives memories of the 1928 Coniston Massacre. The killings occurred in and around the land under claim when Constable William Murray and 'Nugget' Morton led a revenge party through the area following the murder of dingo-trapper Fred Brooks. Although they had nothing to do with the death of Brooks many of those killed were the mothers and fathers of traditional landowners who gave evidence at the land claim hearing. Johnny Nelson Jupurrula's father was taking part in an important ceremony when the revenge party rode along Hanson Creek.

And poor old my old fella, they been make big business. And old fella go round and they didn't know the trouble there. They ran in. They grab them there, make [him] prisoner… they ran into Murray then. Grabem them. Two of them been shot in the Hanson Creek… [After] showing

LAKE NASH

In February 1949, the Alyawarr people at Lake Nash became one of the first groups of Aboriginal pastoral workers in the Northern Territory to strike for wages. The three-month strike ended when management agreed to pay stockmen two pounds a month, plus keep, but living conditions at Lake Nash were still poor.

In the early 1960s the Lake Nash pastoral lease came under the control of the Texas-based King Ranch Incorporated, and by the 1970s the new management was pursuing a deliberate policy of driving traditional landowners off the station by cutting Aboriginal employment and closing the station store to all but station employees.

The Alyawarr had for many years camped near Ilperrlhelame waterhole, an important sacred site which forms part of the Antyipere (Flying Fox), Nyemale (Grass Rat) and Kwerrenye (Green Snake) Dreamings. The camp was just a kilometre from the Lake Nash homestead. The company was determined to see it moved but the Alyawarr were just as determined to remain and look after this important spiritual centre.

The management sent in the bulldozers which tore down a sacred tree, and destroyed the school building, a water tap and the remnants of humpies and then built a fence which cut off about a third of the camp, but the people refused to budge.

The management's harsh policies sparked a national scandal when the Department of Aboriginal Affairs was forced to air drop food and supplies into the community in 1974 after flooding cut the roads and the station refused to sell food to people on the brink of starvation.

Occasional media reports described the degrading conditions and drew graphic pictures of a desolate camp on a bare, dusty flat where Aborigines huddled in derelict cars or in shabby humpies constructed of scrap iron, dry boughs or tattered canvas. There were no working toilets and the water supply consisted of three cold-water taps for a community of about 180. When novelist Xavier Herbert visited Lake Nash in October 1981 he described conditions on the Aboriginal community as 'an insult to the Lord God'.

In 1983 the CLC and other organisations made a concerted effort to force government action on Lake Nash by staging a convoy from Alice Springs to erect shelters at the camp. As political pressure increased the parties resumed negotiations.

Offer and counter-offer were made, until eventually the Alyawarr broke the impasse by agreeing to move to an area about eight kilometres from their present camp if they were assured of unrestricted rights of access to Ilperrlhelame, the store and the airstrip and the relocation of essential services including the school and clinic.

It was not until June 1988 that the Alyawarr finally received freehold title to the excision.

Harry Campbell was one of those who stayed throughout the long struggle:

> *We fought on our own for this country here... We really won this country. They gave it to us, this place here, because we beat them. They [whitefellas] came and fought for the country in the wrong way, as if it was theirs, and tried to make us go back to Sandover country... but we stayed here.*

1981

them all [the rockholes and water] along the country they know. They bin have a chain in the neck, all the way along… When they bin find-em all the people then, last one all right. 'Right you two done it now, you two can get shot.' Bang!

Johnny Nelson Jupurrula giving evidence at the Warlmanpa land claim hearing.

1982

APRIL ➢Justice Toohey retires after five years as Aboriginal Land Commissioner, and is replaced by Justice Sir William Kearney – the former Deputy Chief Justice of the Papua New Guinea Supreme Court.

JUNE ➢Aboriginal Affairs Minister Ian Wilson and Northern Territory Chief Minister Paul Everingham announce a package of amendments to the Land Rights Act. Mr Everingham promotes the Ten-Point Package with a national advertising campaign and a land council delegation travels south to defend land rights.

AUGUST 10–11 ➢The Executives of the Central and Northern Land Councils hold their first joint meeting at Alekarenge. Both councils reaffirm their opposition to the proposed package of amendments.

WOMEN

In early 1982 a delegation of women attended the Central Land Council's meeting in Tennant Creek to put the case for the formation of a Central Australian women's council. The CLC resolved to support the establishment of a women's council, and after extensive consultations in communities throughout Central Australia, women delegates met as the Women's Council Task Force in July 1983 at Basso's Farm, Alice Springs. The meeting discussed how to organise representation from communities and began a process of distributing taped messages to generate discussion and consultation.

A second meeting was held in June 1984 and attended by women from Ernabella to Daguragu. Lena Cavanagh from Santa Teresa summed up the case for a women's council:

> *I think that's good for all women meeting. I want women to be as strong as the men. All the women can get together and have a meeting. Men is too strong on the council, got to be more council ladies strong.*
>
> *All the women can have their own council. They can speak about their land if they want too. They don't have to stand back and let the men do all the talking.*

The Commonwealth Government refused to provide additional funds and a separate women's council was never established.

In recent years there has been renewed interest in the need for women's meetings. Hundreds of women have attended traditional women's law and culturte meetings at Balgo in 1992, Utopia in 1993 and Mt Leibig in 1994.

BARRETT DRIVE

In December 1982 the Northern Territory Government ordered a contractor to blast and bulldoze a sacred site so that Barrett Drive in Alice Springs could be re-aligned to provide better access to the Casino. The desecration occurred without warning in the midst of negotiations with custodians despite a written assurance from the Northern Territory Government that work would not proceed until the issue was resolved.

The sacred site, known as Injalkaljanama, was part of a sacred Caterpillar Dreaming and was registered under the Northern Territory Government's own Aboriginal Sacred Sites Act, but because of a legal loophole charges against then Lands and Housing Minister (now Chief Minister) Marshall Perron had to be dropped.

Mr Perron's actions left a legacy of mistrust:

> *Now it's Marshall Perron — the man who never stops. He never listens for one bit. At Barrett Drive we put up a sign: '$1,000 fine' for somebody doing the wrong thing. That was for a court action.*
> *He never think one bit of it. He just cut off that caterpillar tail. I been go myself and look at the tail! I said 'He don't want a caterpillar's tail. He don't want a cat. He want's to kill them off.'*
> *I asked the Minister, I said to him, he broke his promise.*
> *I told him. 'Look. You know, broken promise by Northern Territory Government by Minister for Land. That's not speaking like that respectful way as a Minister should do. That's not doing a good job for the Territory! He's nothing!'*
> *All those politicians know me. When I was Chairman I keep going protesting up to Darwin and anywhere around here or Tennant Creek, you know.*
> *I don't think there's sacred site protection of Northern Territory Government protection in this country. I'm on the Sacred Sites leadership to tell them what to do. But I don't think they ever take notice. See?*
> *When a problem come. Right oh. Deal with you a good way up front, but bad way behind the back.*
> Wenten Rubuntja 1992

Custodians for the site are deeply upset, not only at the desecration of Injalkaljanama, but also because there was no punishment of those who had broken non-Aboriginal as well as Aboriginal laws. The custodians reported many cases of illness and misfortune as a result of the desecration and, four months after the event, there was record rainfall and flooding of the Todd River. Earth-moving machinery near the site was washed downstream and buried in sand by floodwater.

According to custodian Rosie Furber: 'Those Dreamtime people made those ranges a long time ago, but they are still there. The Dreamtime can still cause problems and hurt people today. It's really dangerous to talk about changing those places because people can get killed.'

1982

SEPTEMBER ➢ Agreement is reached with the Magellan group of companies regarding development of the Palm Valley Gas Field. The agreement includes protection of sacred sites, jobs for Aboriginal people, 'up-front' payments and periodic payments based on the value of production. Another agreement is executed with the Northern Territory Government for lease of the pipeline corridor.

NOVEMBER ➢ The Warumungu land claim hearing begins. Counsel for the Northern Territory Government announces that it has issued leases for several parts of the area under claim to the Northern Territory Land Development Corporation. By leasing the land to its own corporation the Northern Territory Government attempts to alienate the areas and prevent them being claimed. Justice Kearney adjourns the hearing until the issue is settled and the CLC challenges the leases in the High Court.

DECEMBER ➢ A Northern Territory Government contractor blasts and bulldozes a registered sacred site, Injalkaljanama, to clear the way for the re-alignment of Barrett Drive, providing better access to the Alice Springs Casino. The desecration occurs on Boxing Day during negotiations between Government and the site's custodians, and despite Government promises that work would not proceed until the issue was resolved.

LITTLE WELL

In 1982 Little Well soakage – Aluralkwe – was bulldozed and destroyed. The Johnson family had been visiting and camping at Aluralkwe, the only source of good water available in the area, in the hope that they could eventually establish an outstation there.

The soakage was also an important sacred site, part of the Carpet Snake Dreaming. Gregory Johnson was interviewed by ABC radio about the destruction of Aluralkwe:

How long has your family been using that country?
Oh that country they been using for a long time, before me and my families. Before they sink the well down, you see – and that was just a soakage and sacred site. Sacred site, up on the ridge, and they were using it for a long time. Our people, my grandfather, my grandmother's and father's too. And my mother's father.
Did you ask the people on Loves Creek Station if you could go and camp there?
No, we didn't ask them because we belong to that country – we can move out anytime to stop there.
Now, you'd heard there had been some damage to that well. You've been back on the weekend. Tell me what you saw there?
Yeah, saw someone had damaged the well.
How had they damaged it?
With a bulldozer, just covered the well up.
Can you get water out of it now?
No we can't. It's rocky in the well. It's been filled in.
Maybe Aboriginal people did it?
No. They got no bulldozers [laughs]. Somebody else did. White people might be.
Maybe, Aboriginal people have been chasing the bullocks down there, cutting the fences?
No. We didn't cut any fences.
Maybe the station people don't want Aborigines down there?
Yeah. Might be too. Might be I know that already. They don't like the people to stop down there.
How do people feel now they know that well's been filled in?
Pretty worried. A lot of worries for us.

It was later confirmed that Aluralkwe was bulldozed by Loves Creek pastoralist Peter Bloomfield who said he didn't know that it was a sacred site and that he'd bulldozed the soakage to keep Aboriginal people from coming onto his lease (despite the fact that Aboriginal people have a legal right to enter pastoral leases under Northern Territory law).

In 1985 the pastoralist approached the Department of Aboriginal Affairs and agreed to allow the Little Well area to be excised from their lease so that proper outstation facilities could be provided for the families living at the site. In 1992 the Bloomfields sold the lease to Loves Creek to the traditional landowners.

1983

MARCH ➢ The ALP wins the federal election. Bob Hawke becomes Prime Minister. The new Minister for Aboriginal Affairs, Clyde Holding, sets up a National Land Rights Working Party to develop national land rights legislation and in April he meets with the CLC Executive and reiterates the Government's five land rights principles:
- inalienable freehold title for Aboriginal land;
- full legal protection of sacred sites;
- Aboriginal control over mining on Aboriginal land;
- access to mining royalty equivalents; and
- compensation for lost land.

APRIL ➢ Custodians set up a protest camp at Alice Springs Telegraph Station to try and stop the Northern Territory Government's proposal for a recreation lake that would destroy important sacred sites, including Werlatye Atherre. Aboriginal Affairs Minister Clyde Holding proposes a joint Commonwealth–Northern Territory Government Tribunal but Chief Minister Paul Everingham will only agree to the tribunal on certain conditions.

MAY ➢ Representatives of the CLC and other Central Australian organisations meet together to discuss the situation at Lake Nash and other communities trying to establish themselves on pastoral land. Charles Perkins, then head of the Aboriginal Development Corporation, tells the meeting that the Government 'has been mucking around for too long' and promises ADC financial support. The meeting sends a delegation to Lake Nash to consult the community.

JUNE ➢ Clyde Holding appoints former Land Commissioner Justice Toohey to undertake a major review of the Land Rights Act. Toohey takes submissions from the Land Councils, the Commonwealth Government and Territory Government, mining and pastoral bodies, companies and individuals.

At the same time the Burke Government in Western Australia has set up its own Land Rights Inquiry under Paul Seaman QC and promise that, at the very least, they will hand back title to all Aboriginal reserves.

➢ A convoy of vehicles travels from Alice Springs to Lake Nash. The delegation includes representatives from Central Australia's major Aboriginal organisations: Central Australian Aboriginal Media Association, Central Australian Aboriginal Congress, Tangentyere Council and the CLC.

➢ The Mt Barkly land claim hearing is held at Willowra and Mt Barkly before Justice William Kearney.

SEVEN YEARS ON

The election of the Hawke Labor Government in March 1983 rescued the Aboriginal Land Rights Act from the Ten-Point Package, but the pressure from the anti-land rights lobby continued. In June 1983 the new Aboriginal Affairs Minister, Clyde Holding, appointed Justice John Toohey to conduct an inquiry into the Act. Justice Toohey already had five years experience of the Act — he had been appointed as the first Aboriginal Land Commissioner by the Fraser Government.

The terms of reference required Justice Toohey to report and recommend appropriate amendments: to address the needs of dispossessed Aboriginal people who can't claim living areas under the Aboriginal Land Rights Act; to resolve any administrative problems; to reduce any disadvantage that the Act might cause for Aboriginal people; to reduce any areas of conflict between the Aboriginal Land Rights Act and Northern Territory self government; and to consider the extent and type of land available for land claims.

In short he was asked to consider the issues that had been raised in the Northern Territory Government's amendments campaign. All of the major parties, including the Central and Northern Land Councils, the Northern Territory Government and the Commonwealth Government, the Australian Mining Industry Council, the Northern Territory Chamber of Mines and the Northern Territory Cattle Council, made submissions.

Overall Justice Toohey recommended the strengthening and maintenance of the Act. He said there should be no cut off date for land claims, that traditional landowners should retain the right to claim Aboriginal-owned land and pastoral leases and bring repeat claims and that the Northern Territory Government should not be able to alienate land under claim. He recommended that traditional landowners be able to control exploration and mining access to land under claim and that the Act should allow traditional landowners and miners to negotiate agreements that control access at both the exploration and the mining stages.

The Land Councils favoured Commonwealth legislation to protect sacred sites and provide community living areas but Justice Toohey disagreed. He recommended that the Northern Territory Government pass legislation to allow Aboriginal people to claim living areas on pastoral leases, national parks and conservation reserves based on existing or past residence and said the Commonwealth should not override the Northern Territory sacred sites law unless it proved 'demonstrably inadequate'.

Overall Justice Toohey's report strengthened the Aboriginal Land Rights Act and provided a solid defence against those who argued it was a 'social experiment' which had failed:

> *Given the legislative novelty of the subject matter of the Act and the need to marry complex notions of traditional Aboriginal law and culture with European institutions and administrative procedures, the Act has worked surprisingly well. But it is inevitable that after seven years cracks in the edifice have started to show. This report seeks to show how those cracks might be mended while leaving the overall structure intact.*
> Justice Toohey, *Seven Years On.*

1983

JULY ➤ Aboriginal Affairs Minister Clyde Holding says that the Commonwealth Government will act to ensure living areas for Aboriginal people on cattle stations. In comments particularly directed at Lake Nash the Minister says 'This Government does not accept the view that the rights of cattle of some absentee landowners will ever transcend the rights of our indigenous people.' Mr Holding writes to twenty-seven pastoralists urging them to take a sympathetic approach to negotiations over living areas and tells them that if they don't make progress in the next three months he will take unspecified action.

➤ The title to the 4,884 square-kilometre Willowra land claim area is handed back to traditional owners.

➤ Aboriginal Affairs Minister Clyde Holding visits the Alice Springs Telegraph Station protest camp established to stop the Northern Territory Government's proposed recreation lake. He tells the custodians that protection of sacred sites is a matter of Commonwealth concern and they will get the protection of Commonwealth law. His promise is eventually expressed in the Aboriginal and Torres Strait Islander Heritage Protection Act.

AUGUST ➤ A bus takes thirty-one Alyawarr and Warumungu traditional landowners from Tennant Creek to the High Court in Canberra, to hear their case against the Northern Territory Government. At stake is the Northern Territory Government's attempt to stop the Warumungu land claim by leasing part of the land under claim to a Northern Territory Government corporation.

➤ The Central Land Council and traditional landowners sign an agreement with North Flinders Mines for the development of The Granites Gold Mine.

SEPTEMBER ➤ Dr H.C. Coombs presents his final report on the restructuring of the CLC, Executive and organisation to the CLC meeting at Hamilton Downs. In line with the recommendations of the report the CLC elects a new regionally based Executive. At the same meeting Stanley Scrutton is re-elected as Chairman and Kunmanara Breaden is re-elected Deputy Chairman.

OCTOBER ➤ The Commonwealth and Northern Territory Governments establish a board of inquiry to consider the Alice Springs Telegraph Station lake pro-

1983

posal. A fire causes two deaths at the Telegraph Station protest camp and so the campers must move a way as required by Aboriginal law.

➤ The Northern Territory Government introduces the Community Living Areas Bill to address the issue of excisions. The Bill largely reflects the amendment package of two years earlier. The Land Councils oppose the Bill because it makes no promise for Aboriginal people who were forced to leave their land and does not recognise traditional ownership as a basis for claim. The CLC begins legal action in the High Court to prevent the Bill being enacted.

NOVEMBER

➤ The Northern Territory Government alienates Gosse Bluff (Tnorula) by leasing the area to a Northern Territory Government corporation. Tnorala is a sacred site of great significance for Arrernte people who are very concerned to ensure that the area is protected. The lease alienates the

RESTRUCTURING THE CLC

The development of the Central Land Council from a grass-roots organisation is a major source of its strength, but as the CLC's statutory scope and responsibilities grew so did the challenges, and in 1982 Dr. H.C. 'Nugget' Coombs, the former Governor of the Reserve Bank, was brought in to conduct a structural review of the Council.

After eighteen months of consultation, Dr Coombs presented his report to the CLC meeting at Hamilton Downs in September 1983. He recommended that the CLC introduce a new divisional structure co-ordinated through a planning and management committee. Dr Coombs also recommended the adoption of a 'task force' approach to tackle important issues.

By the time of the final report the CLC had already started implementing the recommendations. The Aboriginal Education and Information Division (which later became the CLC Directorate) was established and Patrick Dodson, an Aboriginal man from the Kimberley and former Catholic priest, was appointed as manager.

Coombs recommendations for restructuring the Council and Executive to ensure that they remain representative were also adopted. The Council was expanded to include new communities and the eleven-member Executive was re-organised to include eight members elected to represent specific areas within the CLC region plus the Chairman, the Deputy Chairman and one additional Executive member elected from the Council as a whole.

1983

area and prevents the land from being claimed. The Government keeps the lease a secret for several months and when the traditional landowners learn what has happened they ask the Federal Government to overrule the Northern Territory Government.

➢ The Commonwealth Government announces that it will transfer the title for Uluru National Park to the traditional landowners who will then lease the area back to the Australian National Parks and Wildlife Service.

This is an historic decision and is a measure of the willingness of this Government, on behalf of the Australian people, to recognise the just and legitimate claims of people who have been dispossessed of their land but have never lost their spiritual attachment to the land.
Prime Minister Bob Hawke

Although the transfer has been on the agenda since 1979, Northern Territory Chief Minister Paul Everingham claims that his Government was not consulted: 'It came like a bolt out of the blue — I feel sick in the stomach.' Mr Everingham calls a snap election over the handback decision.

LAND MANAGEMENT

In line with the recommendations of Dr H.C. 'Nugget' Coombs review of the CLC, a land management advisory service for traditional landowners was established in 1983.

The transfer of control over former reserves to Aboriginal people and the success of land claims was generating a growing demand for advice and assistance on land use issues. Establishing 'outstations' or 'homelands' – small family-based communities with only very basic services – was a major priority. Government departments still required traditional landowners to 'prove their commitment' by surviving for months or years without services before they would allow basic facilities to be provided, and the CLC assisted communities to cut through the red tape to reduce these 'probation periods'. There are now more than 200 outstations in the CLC region.

At the same time more established communities were keen to develop commercial land uses: small tourist developments, cattle projects, and feral animal harvesting programs. The land management service — which at first consisted of just two research officers — set out to assist communities to assess development options for their land. Ten years later the CLC's land management service has been expanded to include specialists in land resource assessment, environmental management, business development and the pastoral industry, as well as community development.

1983

➢The Palm Valley gas field is officially opened to supply gas to the Alice Springs powerhouse, one hundred and sixty kilometres away.

➢Justice Toohey completes a review of the Land Rights Act. His report, *Seven Years On,* is submitted to Parliament. The report recommends a strengthening of the Land Rights Act in some areas but the Land Councils are disappointed that Justice Toohey recommends that the Northern Territory Government be allowed to deal with living areas on pastoral land despite their continuing failure to meet Aboriginal needs.

Overall Justice Toohey concludes that the Act is working well.

➢Aboriginal Affairs Minister Holding tells Parliament the Government is determined to see a national land rights package which is consistent with the ALP's five principles. The CLC pushes for national land rights legislation to be at least as strong as the Land Rights Act.

DECEMBER

1984

FEBRUARY ➤ Chief Minister Everingham assures Mr Holding that the Northern Territory Government will legislate for community living areas along the lines advocated in Justice Toohey's report.

PUSHED OFF OUR COUNTRY

The lack of progress on community living areas and excisions has been a source of great frustration for the CLC and traditional owners ever since the Aboriginal Land Rights Act was passed. Many Aboriginal people have been forced off their traditional land by the pastoral industry and forced to move into town or squat without secure title or decent services.

The need for government action to address the needs of these people has been clearly identified by government reports since 1971 when the Gibb Report recommended that these groups be given small excisions on pastoral leases to establish community living areas. But because of opposition from the Cattlemen's Association and the Northern Territory Government very little has been achieved in more than twenty years: Aboriginal people are locked out of the pastoral stations that were built with their labour. The argument for justice was eloquently expressed by one senior Arrernte man:

We worked hard but we got nothing. We've been pushed off our country. We've got to go back there. My poor people they've forgotten their ways today. They've gone mad and lazy. We've got to go back to our country. We've got to make the deaf listen We've got to teach our people.

Tired of waiting, this man and his family set up camp at Undoolya Bore and began squatting on a stock reserve with nothing more than a few tents. Unfortunately this old man died before he saw any land provided for his family.

➤ In a major victory for the CLC, the High Court rules that the Aboriginal Land Commissioner should proceed with the Warumungu land claim despite the Northern Territory Government's attempt to alienate the land under claim. The decision is a victory not just for the Warumungu but also for traditional landowners in other cases where the Northern Territory Government had attempted to prevent land claims by alienating land after a claim was lodged.

➤ Mr Charles Perkins becomes Secretary of the Department of Aboriginal Affairs. Mr Perkins was Chairman of the CLC between September 1975 and June 1976.

1984

➤ A group of five Arrernte families who are traditional landowners for an area of pastoral land north of Alice Springs form the Mpweringe-Arnapipe Outstation Council to press their claims for living areas. The families, who are often referred to as 'the Yambah mob', have been pushing for living areas since 1975.

APRIL

➤ The CLC drafts a policy on excisions markedly different from the Community Living Areas Bill. The policy is designed to deal with the real needs of dispossessed groups and take account of the history which has forced people off their land. It calls for Commonwealth rather than Northern Territory legislation, recognition of traditional affiliation as a factor and Aboriginal freehold title.

➤ The CLC assists traditional landowners in Western Australia to form the Western Desert Land Council, which then makes submissions to the Western Australian Government's land rights inquiry.

MAY

➤ In a widely reported speech, the Executive Director of Western Mining Corporation, Hugh Morgan, describes land rights as a return to paganism and anti-Christian, kicking off a barrage of anti-land rights media. In Western Australia, the mining and pastoral industries mount a scare campaign to influence the Burke Government. The CLC calls on the Commonwealth Government to initiate a public awareness campaign about land rights to dispel the prejudices and misconceptions being exploited by the anti-land rights lobby, but the call is unheeded.

➤ Traditional landowners for Uluru meet with representatives from the Australian National Parks and Wildlife Service, the Conservation Commission of the Northern Territory, the Tourist Commission, the Department of Aboriginal Affairs and the film industry to discuss filming in and around Uluru National Park. The meeting agrees to guidelines which permit most filming but prevent the desecration of sacred sites and intrusions into Aboriginal living areas.

➤ The Arrernte traditional landowners of Yambah Station, north of Alice Springs, meet with John Gorey, the station lessee, to discuss living area excisions. The meeting reaches an in-principle agreement for five small living areas to be provided for the five major families. Unfortunately the death of Mr Gorey and external political pressure mean that the agreement is never honoured.

1984

CLC meets with the Yambah mob prior to meeting with Mr Gorey in May 1984.

JUNE ➢ The Central and Northern Land Councils send a joint delegation to Canberra to meet with Prime Minister Bob Hawke, Aboriginal Affairs Minister Clyde Holding and Resources and Energy Minister Peter Walsh to discuss the mining industry's campaign against land rights. Senator Walsh has already stated publicly that he wants to see mining and exploration speeded up in the Northern Territory and Mr Holding won't commit the Government to maintaining Aboriginal control over mining and exploration on Aboriginal land.

➢ The Commonwealth's *Aboriginal and Torres Strait Islander Heritage (Interim Protection) Act 1984* is passed. The Act protects sites and objects of traditional significance, including human remains. The Act is intended to stay in effect for just two years, as a stop gap until comprehensive land rights and heritage protection legislation can take its place. It is designed to be a 'backstop' when state and territory law fails, and relies on the discretion of the Minister for Aboriginal Affairs. The CLC continues to press for a Commonwealth law giving Aboriginal people real control over sacred sites and cultural heritage.

➢ The Community Living Areas Bill is introduced into the Northern Territory Legislative Assembly, but its passage is tied to another piece of legislation which alienates stock routes and land under claim. The CLC responds by lodging twenty-two land claims to stock routes and stock

RAILWAY

Although the Alice Springs to Darwin railway has still not left the drawing board, traditional landowners gave the project their all clear in 1984.

The Australian National Railway (ANR) approached the Central Land Council in February 1981 for assistance in ensuring that the railway could be constructed without desecrating any sacred sites along the corridor.

The project involved extensive co-operation between the CLC, NLC, Sacred Sites Authority and the ANR, as well as other government departments.

CLC staff were employed to identify traditional landowners and find out from them which areas would need to be protected from railway construction and operations.

In a number of areas the traditional landowners insisted on strong sacred site protection measures but the ANR responded positively and both sides were pleased with the success of the consultations and planning.

'The women were happy about it because they weren't left out like in the past,' said Aboriginal field worker Julie Turner. 'Every time the men were consulted the women were too. Women have separate sites belonging only to them. They need to be consulted separately.'

Former CLC Chairman Wenten Rubuntja, a traditional owner of land affected by the railway, was also pleased:

In our way, Aboriginal way, it's been properly well done. They showed us everything that they wanted to do – which side they wanted to go – which ground they wanted to shift, and we showed them which important place, might be dangerous or sacred place to leave alone. If there's anything more they want to know they can come back again and talk to us, talk to our anthropologists. A good way to do it.

In June 1984 an agreement was reached to ensure that sacred site protection will be written into construction contracts with continuing Aboriginal monitoring and liaison during the work.

OFFICE SPACE

The hostility of the Northern Territory Government to the CLC spilled over from the real issues of land rights to mundane matters like finding proper office space.

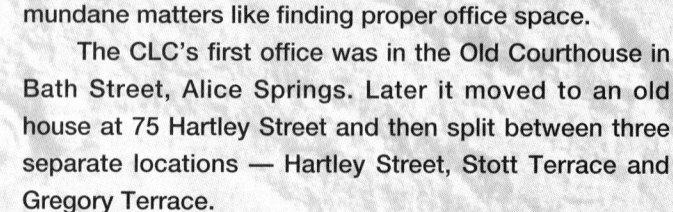

The CLC's first office was in the Old Courthouse in Bath Street, Alice Springs. Later it moved to an old house at 75 Hartley Street and then split between three separate locations — Hartley Street, Stott Terrace and Gregory Terrace.

Co-ordinating the office in three different locations was a major problem. By 1984 CLC was looking to bring all its operation under one roof and it agreed to purchase the Diarama Village on the western side of Alice Springs. To proceed with the purchase CLC needed to have a minor rezoning application approved so that the complex could be used as office space rather than as shops. It seemed to be only a technicality, but the Northern Territory Planning Authority rejected the application after holding a secret hearing to listen to objections. The CLC was surprised not only by the decision but also by the way that the matter had been dealt with. The CLC was not given a chance to put its case and neither the Planning Authority or the Minister for Lands Marshall Perron would reveal the reasons for the decision nor respond to CLC inquiries.

The matter eventually went to the Supreme Court which ruled that CLC had been denied natural justice and quashed Mr Perron's decision, but by then it was too late for the sale to go through.

After the Stott Terrace office was destroyed by fire in March 1985, the CLC opened an office in Parsons Street and in August that year applied to have a complex on the Stuart Highway rezoned for office use. Although the site had been zoned light industrial since 1981, Northern Territory Government departments had been using it as office space for five years. The rezoning was opposed by local CLP member Roger Vale and others, on the grounds that it might attract Aboriginal people to the area, but this time the Planning Authority approved the rezoning and the CLC finally consolidated its operations under one roof in February 1986.

Hartley Street.

Stott Terrace

Gregory Terrace

Stuart Highway

1984

reserves alongside leases where pastoralists have not co-operated with excisions negotiations. The Cattlemen's Association urges its members to stop negotiations altogether and Mr Holding calls a meeting with representatives of CLC, NLC, DAA, the cattlemen and the Northern Territory Government.

JULY

➢The Yambah mob decide to move out of town and live on stock route and stock reserve areas near Yambah Station, north of Alice Springs. They hope that by camping on their traditional land they can increase the pressure for some suitable excisions.

This is my father's land. That is why I am stopping here. With white man's land, when the station owner dies, his son takes over. It's just the same. This is my father's land and I'm taking over.
All we want is our place.
Silas Turner

AUGUST

➢The Board of Inquiry into the proposed Alice Springs Telegraph Station recreation lake accepts the significance of the sacred sites which would be destroyed and highlights engineering problems of the proposal. The Northern Territory Government says it will look at alternatives, but Chief Minister Everingham says the Telegraph Station may be considered again.

➢At a meeting to resolve the crisis over the Community Living Areas Bill, Mr Holding proposes formation of a working party on the stock routes and reserves claims. He says the Federal Government will act if the Northern Territory Government doesn't pass excisions legislation in line with Justice Toohey's recommendations.

SEPTEMBER

➢The Western Australian Government gives in to pressure from the mining industry and abandons recommendations of Commissioner Seaman's inquiry into land rights in Western Australia. While Prime Minister Bob Hawke is flying to Perth, Premier Brian Burke announces unilaterally that there will be no national land rights legislation. Burke's backdown splits the ALP in the run-up to the federal election, and although Labor wins the November election, Prime Minister Hawke endorses Premier Burke's retreat from the mining veto during the campaign.

OCTOBER

➢In order to speed up the land claim process a second Aboriginal Land Commissioner, Justice Michael Maurice, is appointed. He and Justice Kearney will divide the workload to try and clear the backlog of claims waiting to be heard.

1984

➤ The CLC assists in the establishment of the Jurnkurakurr Outstation Resource Centre to serve traditional landowners in the Tennant Creek region.

DECEMBER ➤ The Northern Territory Government informs the Land Councils that it is not prepared to proceed with the Community Living Areas Bill, after more than a year of negotiations on the issue.

➤ Agreement is reached with Mereenie Joint Venturers regarding an easement for, and access roads to, the Mereenie–Alice Springs oil pipeline crossing more than 200 kilometres of Aboriginal land. In addition, CLC commits substantial resources to investigating the possible commercial participation of traditional owners in a proposed pipeline to Yulara Village.

The Mereenie–Alice Springs pipeline being laid.

1985

FEBRUARY

➢ The Hawke Government announces its revamped Preferred National Land Rights Model. The model is a 'set of principles' to which the Commonwealth believes all territory, state and Commonwealth legislation should conform. Four of the five 'principles' that the Government outlined in March 1983 have been dumped. The new model:

- requires no Aboriginal consent for mining on Aboriginal land,
- prevents land claims over stock routes, stock reserves and Aboriginal-owned pastoral leases, and
- restricts eligibility for excisions.

The National Federation of Land Councils and the National Aboriginal Conference walk out of the next Land Rights Working Party meeting in protest. The chairmen of the Northern Territory Land Councils — Stan Scrutton of the CLC, Galarrwuy Yunupingu of the Northern Land Council and Jimmy Tipungwuti of the Tiwi Land Council — tour every major Aboriginal community in the Territory to discuss the implications of the Preferred Model. *Our Land is Our Life*, the first land rights documentary made by a Northern Territory Aboriginal organisation, is produced during the tour to carry the message nationally.

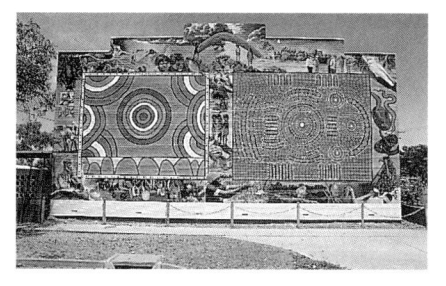

MARCH

➢ The CLC opens an office in Tennant Creek. It is the Central Land Council's first office outside Alice Springs and an important step towards regionalisation and improved access for traditional landowners throughout Central Australia.

➢ The Warumungu land claim hearing resumes under Justice Maurice. Fourteen separate portions of land are claimed by eleven local descent groups. Within a year, the Warumungu land claim will be the subject of three separate legal actions brought by the Northern Territory Government. Processing of land claims slows to a halt as legal actions in this and other land claims move through the courts.

WARUMUNGU

The story of the Warumungu people and their fight for land rights cannot be properly presented in this small book. The early white explorers described the Warumungu as a flourishing nation in the 1870s, but by 1915 the onslaught of invasion and reprisal had brought them to the brink of starvation.

The reserve that was set aside for the Warumungu in 1892 was revoked in 1934 to make way for gold prospectors and they were shunted to new reserves which were later also revoked until by the 1960s they were pushed off their traditional land altogether.

But the Warumungu would not give up. They made their first written application for land in 1975 when the Rockhampton Downs Aboriginal community asked for their land back so they could run their own affairs. In 1978 the CLC lodged a claim under the Aboriginal Land Rights Act on behalf of the Warumungu. Their claim was one of the longest and hardest fought in the history of the Act.

The Northern Territory tried to prevent the claim from proceeding by changing the status of the land under claim. Land within town boundaries cannot be claimed, so in 1978 the Government enlarged the town boundaries of Tennant Creek to cover 750 square kilometres — the size of a major city. Land which has been alienated — sold or leased — cannot be claimed, so in 1982 the Government leased nine of the twelve areas under claim to a government-controlled corporation — a fact that they announced two days after the start of the hearing before Justice William Kearney in November 1982.

The resulting litigations went all the way to the High Court and the hearing did not resume until March 1985 — this time before Aboriginal Land Commissioner Michael Maurice.

Maurice recommended the return of a large part of the claim in July 1988 — ten years after the claim was lodged. It was another three years before any part of the land was handed back and five years before most was returned.

Although the land had been recommended for grant the claimants were required to negotiate with other land users, such as Tennant Creek Town Council, pastoralists, businesses and the Northern Territory Government, to ensure their interests weren't adversely affected. The major issue was the land adjacent to the Tennant Creek town boundary: the claimants offered to give up a large area of this land in return for control over some important sacred sites. While the Town Council was willing to accept this offer, the Northern Territory Government was not and the negotiations dragged on for more than three years.

Most of the land was handed back in four stages between May 1991 and July 1993.

When the town boundary areas were returned in March 1993 former Aboriginal Land Commissioner Michael Maurice was asked to look back at the Warumungu land claim:

> *The problem with the Northern Territory Government then... was it didn't accept the underlying principles of the Aboriginal Land Rights Act. It didn't accept that it was for the Commonwealth to determine the conditions on which Aboriginal people could acquire land in the Northern Territory, so its attitude was one of resistance.*

1985

➢ The CLC's office in Stott Terrace, Alice Springs, is destroyed by fire. The Stott Terrace office housed the CLC's library and registry divisions and many valuable files are destroyed.

Photo: *Centralian Advocate*

➢ Chief Minister Ian Tuxworth announces that the Northern Territory will not introduce any excisions legislation and instead produces a set of 'administrative guidelines' which will form the basis for handling all excision applications. Under the guidelines even fewer families will be eligible than under the discarded Community Living Areas Bill. The CLC objects vigorously, but Aboriginal Affairs Minister Clyde Holding suggests that the CLC assess the guidelines after six months in operation. During the next year, CLC assists Aboriginal groups in negotiations for living areas and for excisions on fifty-nine stations while continuing to pursue stock-route land claims.

APRIL

➢ Traditional landowners purchase McLaren Creek pastoral station with funding from the Aboriginals Benefit Trust Account and legal support from CLC. The station is run down and virtually de-stocked but will give access to land and sacred sites to people dispossessed for generations. Plans are to restore it to a working cattle station and the traditional owners trap and sell the feral horses that have overrun the station to finance this development. The CLC lodges a land claim for the station immediately.

In 1985 we bought this McLaren Creek Station and you know when I first came to this place there was nothing. No cattle, nothing. Just place.

53

1985

That was three years ago. No horses for riding, nothing.
Now we claim this country because it's our father's country. We've been working on stations all our life, working for someone else. Now we can work for ourselves.
I've been working hard battling for something.
Getting our land back means we can carry on and our children can carry on after us. That's the way we want it – to look after everything and do a good job. We're still doing it the olden-time way. Go around with the horses checking up the waterholes and fixing the bores. Now there's no white man looking after the bores, we've got to do it ourselves.
We had a meeting and they picked me to be manager because I understand cattle. We've got to do all this fencing around the paddock now and clean it up and fix the bore and then go and look for cattle again.
You know, you can't do all that in one day.

Murphy Jappanangka, Station Manager, McLaren Creek

MAY ➤More than 1,000 Aboriginal people march on Parliament House in Canberra to protest against the Preferred National Land Rights Model. The CLC's Patrick Dodson attacks Mr Holding's policies and the Preferred Model at a National Press Club luncheon. At first Prime Minister Bob Hawke refuses to answer their calls for a meeting, but later agrees to meet a delegation although little progress is made.

Photo: L.Graham

➤Aboriginal Land Commissioner William Kearney recommends that the entire Mt Barkly land claim area be returned to the traditional owners.

1985

JUNE

➢ The Northern Territory Government announces that $1.5 million will be cut from minor community funding, which will severely affect outstations and pastoral excision communities. CLC vows that the 'return to the land' will continue despite the cutbacks.

➢ The CLC, Tangentyere Council and Central Australian Aboriginal Congress establish the Centrecorp Aboriginal Investment Corporation. Centrecorp is owned on behalf of all Aboriginal people in Central Australia to raise money for investment in resource development and tourism projects on Aboriginal land, to create longer term economic security for traditional landowners.

JULY

➢ Aboriginal Affairs Minister Clyde Holding hands back title for the 2,590-square-kilometre Mt Barkly land claim area to the traditional owners.

SEPTEMBER

➢ *Land Rights News* becomes a fully fledged newspaper jointly published by the Central, Northern and Tiwi Land Councils. The newspaper replaces the old *Central Australian Land Rights News* and a similar NLC newsletter.

➢ A spokesman for cattlemen in central Australia, Mr Grant Heaslip, says on ABC TV that if legislation is passed requiring pastoralists to grant excisions, blood would be shed.

OCTOBER

➢ Kunmanara Breaden takes over as Acting Chairman of the CLC following the resignation of Stan Scrutton. Mr Breaden has been Deputy Chairman since December 1980.

➢ The six-month trial period ends for the excision guidelines, and not one Crown Term Lease has been signed.

➢ The Central Land Council authorises development of a 'field division' with a separate manager and community-based information officers supported by town-based personnel to improve communication between CLC and the communities.

OCTOBER 26

➢ Title to the 1,325-square-kilometre Uluru–Kata Tjuta National Park is handed back to the traditional landowners by Governor-General Sir Ninian Stephen. Aboriginal people from throughout Australia attend the

NATIONAL LAND RIGHTS

When the Hawke Government came to power in 1983 it promised strong national land rights based on the standard established in the Northern Territory. Two years later Aboriginal organisations were confronted with a weakened Preferred Model for National Land Rights that would undercut the Aboriginal Land Rights Act. For Aboriginal people in states like Queensland, Tasmania and Western Australia it was an inadequate offer, but for the traditional owners of the Northern Territory it threatened to wind back the clock.

The Northern Territory Land Councils were united in their opposition to the proposal. In just two weeks the chairmen of the Central, Northern and Tiwi Land Councils travelled thousands of kilometres to inform and consult every major Aboriginal community in the Northern Territory. 'The response of Aboriginal people was adamant', reported CLC Chairman Stan Scrutton. 'We must fight to keep the old law, and do everything possible to stop the Labor Government from destroying existing rights.'

Only the concerted efforts of Aboriginal groups from all around the country prevented the weakened model from being imposed. A convoy of buses, Land Cruisers and a truck carried 200 people from Alice Springs to Canberra to join a thousand others in the first land rights protest in the national capital for over ten years. They marched on Parliament House and later occupied the office of Charles Perkins, then Secretary of the Department of Aboriginal Affairs, demanding to speak to Prime Minister Bob Hawke and Aboriginal Affairs Minister Clyde Holding. Eventually Mr Hawke agreed to postpone the legislation to allow further consultations.

Ten months later the Commonwealth abandoned its national land rights legislation.

Unfortunately it was a victory for the miners and pastoralists and state governments rather than the Land Councils. The Hawke Government had decided to leave land rights legislation to the states. The imminent threat of the Preferred Model was gone but the land rights movement was on the defensive and the Aboriginal Land Rights (Northern Territory) Act was under threat.

Photo: L. Graham

1985

ceremony but not the Northern Territory's Chief Minister Ian Tuxworth. He reiterates the Northern Territory Government's opposition to the handover.

My grandmother, father, mother, uncle and brothers all knew this place. But when the white man came he didn't know the Law or the sacred places. He didn't know what he was doing. His law is in a book. Aboriginal people don't need books to know the Law. The white man came with camels and he looked at Uluru, but he didn't see. He thought there was nothing but the Rock. He has no understanding of the Law of the country. He broke everything, broke the Aboriginal Law completely.

Now they're beginning to learn. Now we are working together. Now we're level. Anangu [Aboriginal people] are happy for the whitefella to come here but they have to obey the Law.

Tony Tjamiwa, Uluru Board member

NOVEMBER

➤ The Commonwealth drafts amendments to weaken the Land Rights Act and make it consistent with the Preferred National Land Rights Model. The Australian Mining Industry Council launches a national campaign alleging that Land Councils are a menace to national economic recovery and that the 'experiment' in the Northern Territory hasn't worked. CLC works to refute these arguments throughout 1986.

➤ Former CLC Chairman Wenten Rubuntja is again elected as Chairman and Geoff Shaw is elected as Deputy Chairman. The CLC administration is reorganised and Patrick Dodson is appointed to the newly created position of CLC director.

DECEMBER

➤ The Northern Territory Government's *Crown Lands Amendment Act (No. 2) 1985* comes into effect. The new law removes long-standing Aboriginal rights to reside on pastoral land. These rights had been guaranteed since the pastoral industry began in the 1860s but the Commonwealth Government refuses to override the amendments. The CLC believes the changes are designed to prevent traditional landowners from strengthening their claims for excisions on pastoral land.

ULURU HANDBACK

The handback of Uluru in October 1985 was a symbolic highpoint for land rights. The area around Uluru and Kata Tjuta was alienated after the Aboriginal Land Rights Act was passed by the declaration of the Uluru and Kata Tjuta (Ayers Rock–Mt Olga) National Park in 1977. Justice Toohey ruled in April 1979 that this prevented any land claim over the Park because it transferred title for the land to the Director of the Australian National Parks and Wildlife Service.

The Park could only become Aboriginal land if the Commonwealth amended the Land Rights Act, and representations from the CLC and traditional landowners to the then Prime Minister Malcom Fraser and Aboriginal Affairs Minister Fred Chaney began almost immediately. The traditional landowners wanted title to the land and majority Aboriginal representation on the Park's board of management. They agreed to lease the park area back to the Australian National Parks and Wildlife Service (ANPWS) which would maintain day-to-day responsibility for running the Park.

Uluru is a powerful symbol and the traditional landowners had strong support throughout the country from organisations like the National Aboriginal Congress, but they were also facing trenchant opposition from the Northern Territory Government.

The CLC and the Pitjantjatjara Council worked closely together organising numerous meetings to consult the traditional landowners and consider offers and counter offers from the Commonwealth Government and Northern Territory Government.

Negotiations crystallised the different positions: the traditional landowners wanted inalienable freehold title under the Aboriginal Land Rights Act, with a lease to ANPWS and an Aboriginal majority on the board; the Northern Territory Government wanted title transferred from the Commonwealth to the Northern Territory Government which would give some reduced form of title to the traditional owners with Aboriginal people involved in park management but not in control.

The stalemate continued until the Hawke Government came to power in 1983 and in November of that year Bob Hawke announced that his government would amend the Aboriginal Land Rights Act to return the title for Uluru–Kata Tjuta National Park to the traditional landowners.

Hundreds of Aboriginal and non-Aboriginal people attended the handback on 26 October 1985 when Governor-General Sir Ninian Stephen handed over the title papers at a ceremony near the base of Uluru. Five minutes later the traditional landowners signed an agreement leasing the Park back to the ANPWS.

The Northern Territory Government was so angered by the handover that it withdrew from the management arrangements and the Park is now run jointly by the traditional landowners and the Australian Nature Conservation Agency (the renamed ANPWS).

1986

➤ The Commonwealth Government abandons its own national land rights legislation but not proposed amendments to weaken land rights in the Northern Territory. In the face of a public scare campaign by the mining industry and the backdown by the Western Australian Labor Party, the Government retreats from its own commitments feebly claiming that most states have made 'advances' towards land rights.

MARCH

➤ The CLC organises an intensive uranium education program, including a three-day tour of the Ranger Uranium Mine, to help traditional landowners make informed decisions about mining exploration in the Tanami Desert. Several companies then present exploration proposals to the traditional landowners.

APRIL

➤ Twenty years after the Gurindji walkoff sparked the modern struggle for land rights, the Gurindji are given inalienable freehold title to Daguragu under the Land Rights Act.

➤ Aboriginal Affairs Minister Clyde Holding hands back the title of 60,000 square kilometres to the Karlantijpa Land Trusts at Yankirrikirlangu, 190 kilometres west of Tennant Creek. The area is made up of land returned under the Warlmanpa and Kaytej–Warlpiri land claims.

➤ The Commonwealth Government still proposes amendments to the Land Rights Act even though the National Land Rights Model has now been dropped. The amendments would effectively remove the Aboriginal consent for mining on Aboriginal land and prevent land claims over stock routes and Aboriginal-owned pastoral leases. The CLC lobbies intensely to defend the Act.

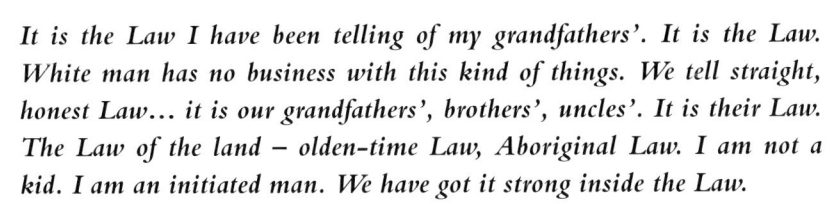

It is the Law I have been telling of my grandfathers'. It is the Law. White man has no business with this kind of things. We tell straight, honest Law... it is our grandfathers', brothers', uncles'. It is their Law. The Law of the land – olden-time Law, Aboriginal Law. I am not a kid. I am an initiated man. We have got it strong inside the Law.
Peter Kanari, Lake Amadeus land claim

1986

JUNE ➢ Traditional landowners and representatives of major Australian business firms exchange eight leases and access and equity agreements in relation to the Palm Valley to Darwin pipeline. The pipeline will travel through more than 700 kilometres of Aboriginal land in the CLC areas. The Aboriginal investment company Centrecorp acquires 1.4 per cent of Northern Territory Gas and the pipeline.

➢ The Aboriginal Land Commissioner Michael Maurice recommends that most of the Ti-Tree land claim be granted, but rules that a 1.6-kilometre stock route across the former station is a public road which cannot be granted. The stock route area contains sacred sites and cuts the station in half. Excluding it from the grant would make the station unworkable and the traditional owners apply to the Federal Court for a review of the Commissioner's decision.

➢ The *Aboriginal and Torres Strait Islander (Interim Protection) Act 1984* is amended. In 1984 Aboriginal Affairs Minister Clyde Holding told Parliament the Act 'would be replaced by more comprehensive legislation dealing with Aboriginal land rights and heritage protection'. The Act was supposed to expire naturally through a 'sunset clause' that gave it a two-year life but now the Government simply removes the sunset clause and the word 'Interim Protection' from the Act's title and it continues to operate. The CLC and other organisations are disappointed that the Act leaves the protection of sacred sites up to ministerial discretion rather than making it mandatory.

AUGUST ➢ The Northern Territory Government establishes a committee, chaired by Solicitor-General Brian Martin, to review the operation of the Aboriginal Sacred Sites Protection Authority. The committee, which does not include any Aboriginal people, is asked to make recommendations regarding the Northern Territory legislation to 'protect areas which are sacred or otherwise of significance to Aboriginals'.

➢ The Northern Territory Minister for Mines and Energy, Barry Coulter, proposes the establishment of a toxic waste incinerator near Warrego, west of Tennant Creek. The Aboriginal and non-Aboriginal residents of the Tennant Creek region join forces against the proposal and the Northern Territory Government backs down.

1986

OCTOBER

➤ The CLC and other Aboriginal organisations convince the Commonwealth to revamp proposed amendments to the Land Rights Act. Amendments to the mining section are deferred so that the views of Aboriginal groups can be properly considered.

➤ Agreement is reached in principle with the Commonwealth Minister for Communications to transfer title to 5.3 hectares of Telecom land at the old Barrow Creek Telegraph Station reserve to the Kaytetye people to set up a store, resource centre and museum.

DECEMBER

➤ The 1,700-kilometre Palm Valley–Darwin Pipeline is opened ahead of schedule. The CLC believes the success of this and other projects will show people that development can occur on Aboriginal land to the benefit of all Territorians.

HEAR OUR CALL

When Pope John Paul visited Australia in 1986 he asked the Australian Catholic Church to arrange a national event where he could address the Aboriginal and Torres Strait Islander people of Australia. Alice Springs was chosen as the venue and the CLC played a major role in the organisation of the Pope's visit.

CLC Chairman Wenten Rubuntja was commissioned to paint a large canvas which was presented to the Pope along with a message shield calling for his help in seeking a just settlement for Aboriginal people:

We the indigenous people of Australia call for justice as owners and occupiers of this country.

Our Being is in the Land. We belong to it as it always belonged to us, but the integrity of our culture, our economy, our relationship with the Land has been denied since the invasion of 1788. ...Peace and justice can only be achieved if the lie of 'terra nullius' and the injustices that it continues to create are destroyed.

HEAR OUR CALL

Your Church had played a part in our dispossession and oppression. Your visit gives you the opportunity to add your voice to our 200-year struggle for peace and justice.

On behalf of our ancestors and the children still to be born we expect you to heed our call for reconciliation and justice.

On 29 November hundreds of Aboriginal people from all over Australia gathered in Alice Springs to hear the Pope offer his support in the fight for justice:

You have learned how to survive, whether on your own lands, or scattered among the towns and cities. Though you difficulties are not yet over, you must learn to draw on the endurance which your ancient ceremonies have taught you. Take heart from the fact that many of your languages are still spoken and that you still possess your ancient culture. You have kept your sense of brotherhood. If you stay closely united you are like a tree standing in the middle of a bushfire sweeping through the timber. The leaves are scorched and the tough bark is scarred and burnt; but inside the tree the sap is still flowing, and under the ground the roots are still strong. Like the tree you have endured the flames, and you still have the power to be reborn. The time for this rebirth is now!

Let it not be said that the fair and equitable recognition of Aboriginal rights to land is discrimination. To call for the acknowledgement of the land rights of people who have never surrendered those rights is not discrimination. Certainly what has been done cannot be undone. But what can now be done to remedy the deeds of yesterday must not be put off until tomorrow.

Photo: Di Calder

1987

FEBRUARY

➤The Warumungu land claim resumes after a two-year delay caused by Northern Territory Government legal challenges. The Tennant Creek Town Council accepts the claimants' offer to withdraw more than ninety per cent of their claim over land close to town, but the Northern Territory Government rejects the offer and files an application in the Federal Court to have Land Commissioner Maurice disqualified from hearing the claim.

By this date, the Northern Territory Government has been to the High, Federal and Northern Territory Supreme Courts on twenty-four separate occasions in relation to land claims. The courts have ruled for the Northern Territory Government in only one case.

MARCH

➤Two eminent prehistorians estimate the Aboriginal population at the time of the First Fleet was between 750,000 and 1,300,000, and that more than 600,000 Aboriginal people died as a result of the British invasion.

➤The Federal Parliamentary Inquiry into Aboriginal Homelands urges state and federal government support for the growing outstation movement through the provision of basic facilities to more than 500 small, remote Aboriginal communities.

Two months later the Northern Territory Government announces that Aboriginal communities with populations of less than fifty are not entitled to government assistance other than water supplies. About six per cent of the Northern Territory population is affected by this decision.

APRIL

➤The CLC assists Ipolera outstation near Hermannsburg to become the first community to open a small tourist venture. The venture attracts government and commercial support.

➤The Northern Territory Government again loses its court action when the full bench of the Federal Court says that Aboriginal Land Commissioner Maurice may hear the Warumungu land claim. Hearing resumes but the claim is still subject to continuing legal actions by the Northern Territory Government.

➤The *Northern Territory Trespass Act 1987* is passed, making it easier to forcibly remove Aboriginal people from stock routes without a judicial hearing.

MAY

➤Mingatjuta Development Pty Ltd, a joint venture of Centrecorp and Northern Territory tour operator Bill King, leases part of Watarrka (Kings Canyon) National Park to set up a wilderness lodge.

1987

➢ At a historic joint meeting at Lake Bennett, south of Darwin, the Central and Northern Land Councils agree to amendments to the Land Rights Act. The compromise package:

- preserves the traditional landowners rights to control access for mining and exploration but ties the two activities together so that an acceptance of exploration means an acceptance of mining;
- imposes a strict one-year negotiation limit for applications;
- introduces a provision for a government-appointed arbitrator to settle disputes over exploration and mining agreements; and
- sets a deadline on land claims so that no claim can be lodged after June 1997.

It will be a national disgrace if the two-hundredth year of our dispossession passes without the proper recognition of our indigenous rights as the traditional owners of Australia.
The time is well overdue for our rights to be recognised by a national treaty, or embedded in the Australian constitution, and for the extension of existing rights to all parts of Australia.
We cannot continue to witness the spectacle of our limited land rights being subjected to the pressures that can be brought to bear on the parliamentary process.
1988 will be a test of Australia's political leadership both in Australia and the international arena.
CLC Director Pat Dodson, speaking at the Federation of Land Councils meeting in Alice Springs, June 1987

JUNE ➢ The *Aboriginal Land Rights (Northern Territory) Amendment Act 1987* receives assent on 5 June. The Northern Territory Department of Mines and Energy responds to the amendments with a flood of Exploration Lease Applications which it had withheld while waiting for the changes.

➢ Final evidence is heard in the Warumungu land claim. Two months later, final written submissions are received. It is nine years since the claim was first lodged.

➢ The Martin Committee delivers its report on sacred sites protection to the Chief Minister. The Committee recommends major changes which would give the Minister for Lands the power to override the Authority and authorise the desecration or destruction of sacred sites.

1987 AMENDMENTS

The Northern Territory Land Councils had taken a leading role in the fight against the Hawke Government's weakened National Land Rights Model in 1985 but the abandonment of the model did not ease the pressure on the *Aboriginal Land Rights (Northern Territory) Act*.

In April 1986 Aboriginal Affairs Minister Clyde Holding announced that the Act would be amended to prevent land claims over Aboriginal-owned pastoral properties as well as stock routes and reserves, to give the Northern Territory Government new powers to compulsorily acquire Aboriginal land for public purposes, and to remove traditional landowners' control over mining and other developments on Aboriginal land.

The Land Councils lobbied intensely to defend their rights. There were delegations to the Labor Party, the Coalition and the Democrats. They lobbied the institutions which finance mining projects, and received strong support from the trade union movement, the Churches, the Federation of Ethnic Community Councils, international indigenous rights organisations and the Federal Labor Party's Caucus Committee on Aboriginal Affairs.

By November 1986 it seemed the campaign to defend land rights had succeeded. The Commonwealth withdrew the amendments and assured the Land Councils that the proposals were 'on the back-burner'. Five months later they were back in the flame.

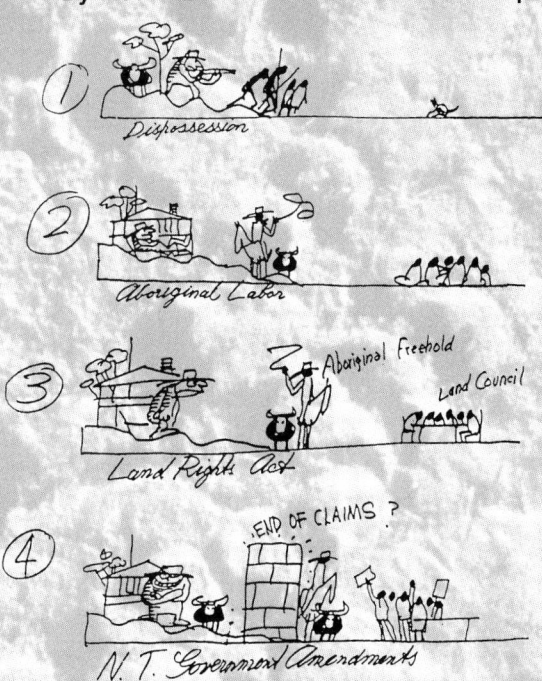

The Northern Territory Government and the mining industry kept up the heat by arguing that the Act was causing a 'log-jam' for exploration applications and produced statistics to support their case. The truth of the matter was that the Northern Territory Government and some mining companies were deliberately dragging their feet to increase the political pressure for amendments: between July 1986 and June 1987 the Northern Territory Minister for Mines and Energy approved only one of the twenty or more exploration applications before his department. Without his approval the applications could not be considered by the CLC.

These tactics succeeded in spite of the facts and the Land Councils were forced to accept a compromise package of amendments.

The package was presented to a meeting of the Central and Northern Land Councils in May 1987 by Resources and Energy Minister Gareth Evans. The joint council meeting accepted the amendment package which was then passed into law in June 1987.

1987

JULY ➢ The CLC assists Areyonga Community to get funding and equipment for a project to capture feral horses to break in, breed and sell. The project provides employment and training for young Aboriginal people on the community.

➢ In a national election the Australian Labor Party retains Government. Gerry Hand, a former member of the Labor Party Caucus Committee on Aboriginal Affairs, replaces Clyde Holding as Minister for Aboriginal Affairs.

➢ Initial agreement is reached between the lessee of Aileron Station and traditional owners regarding an excision of five square kilometres. It has been nearly twenty years since the Aileron group first tried to negotiate an excision. Unfortunately, they become stuck in a new catch-22 situation when the Northern Territory Lands Department refuses to issue title until water is found while the Northern Territory Power and Water Authority won't drill for water until the title is issued.

SEPTEMBER ➢ During an interview at the Central Australian Aboriginal Media Association (CAAMA) in Alice Springs, Prime Minister Bob Hawke says he wants to make a treaty with Aboriginal people.

I want to see an understanding in the Australian community that we have an obligation to the Aborigines of Australia – that in 200 years of European settlement there have been many grave injustices done. I think that as a people we ought to make a contract between one another.
I don't think we should be hung up on the words. The important thing is that there be a clear statement of understanding by the total Australian community of the obligations that the community has to rectify so many of the injustices that have accumulated over 200 years.
Prime Minister Bob Hawke, 2 September 1987

➢ Aboriginal Affairs Minister Gerry Hand establishes a working party on stock route claims and excisions. The Central and Northern Land Councils, the Department of Aboriginal Affairs and the Northern Territory Government are all represented, but the Northern Territory Cattlemen's Association refuses to participate.

OCTOBER ➢ The CLC assists with the incorporation of Ngurratjuta Air Pty Ltd. The new airline is partly funded from royalty equivalents earned from mining on Aboriginal land and provides a light plane service to Aboriginal communities in Central Australia.

WE ALL BELONG TO THE SONGS

When the English people found our country and Aboriginal people, they put their cities and their culture all over our country.

But underneath this, all the time, Aboriginal culture and laws stay alive.

In Central Australia, everyone knows this, they can see our culture, our laws, and the song in the land has a voice – the Warlpiri voice, the Arrernte, the Luritja, the Pitjantjatjara, the Warumungu, the Alyawarr, Gurindji, Pintupi – many voices.

And while we have been keeping the Law, we've had to make relations with Europeans and European law.

At first we stirred each other up, then we learnt we had to live together. We now get our protection from the Australian Government and we negotiate. We must negotiate as equals – we have got to have that balance.

So it goes on the same for us whether it is 100 years or 200 or 300 – there's the Australian community, the Australian Government, Australian culture, and then there is Aboriginal culture, our leaders, and our Law, and we are together in the one country. We are all Australian citizens now.

We are going to show people from overseas, and from all over Australia, just how strong our spirit is, that we have survived, through our culture and our Law, and that it was us Aboriginal people, and our fathers, mothers and grandparents who did this. Europeans didn't even notice, they did not care. They even thought our culture might die out.

So when we have our cultural festival up here in the Centre and then up the Top End, some time in the middle of the year, we will show everyone our culture, and they will have the chance to learn something.

And for Aboriginal people living along the coast when they white people took over first, they will be able to see that they are still part of the Aboriginal family.

People down there might not know their language any more, but the Emu Story and the Snake Story goes all over Australia.

They are all descended from the Emu and Snake Stories that come across from the sea, through Arrernte country here, and all of them go through Uluru and Kata Tjuta. Aboriginal people in Port Augusta, way down in South Australia, they are descendants of the Two-Women Story. That comes all the way up here, too. We will be able to show them this.

We will have our ceremonies at Uluru and Kata Tjuta – the people who were born in the country will introduce the visitors from the Top End, from Arrernte and Warlpiri country, and the ones that have come from the coast and the cities.

When they see us dance we can celebrate that we all belong to the songs that go across the whole of this country.

CLC Chairman Wenten Rubuntja

1987

NOVEMBER ➤ The Central, Northern and Tiwi Land Councils and Pitjantjatjara Council meet together and decide to boycott the Bicentennial celebrations. They believe that the anniversary of white settlement provides little for Aboriginal people to celebrate and decide to spend the year celebrating the survival of Aboriginal culture.

➤ The full bench of the Federal Court finds that stock routes are not public roads and are therefore claimable under the Land Rights Act. This issue had led to Northern Territory Government legal actions in five land claims in the CLC area. The Northern Territory Government unsuccessfully applies for special leave to appeal to the High Court.

DECEMBER ➤ In a speech to Parliament, Aboriginal Affairs Minister Gerry Hand announces an intensive round of consultation with Aboriginal organisations Australia-wide to discuss reorganisation of Aboriginal and Islander affairs under a national Aboriginal and Torres Strait Islanders Commission (ATSIC) based on elected regional councils. Development of a treaty or compact between Aboriginal and non-Aboriginal Australians is also part of the plan.

➤ Justice William Kearney retires as Aboriginal Land Commissioner. The new Aboriginal Land Commissioner will take up his appointment in May 1988.

1988

JANUARY

➤CLC members travel in a convoy with Aboriginal people from the Top End and the Kimberley to march in Sydney on Australia Day where an estimated 20,000 Aboriginal people join their supporters from the trade unions, the churches, ethnic groups and the wider community, in a demonstration of survival.

A joint statement signed by the heads of fourteen churches calls for Aboriginal rights, including a secure land base.

Oh no... ...International Terrorists!

➤More than twenty excisions applications are submitted to the Northern Territory Lands Department. For most of the year the Department fails to take the steps outlined in its own administrative guidelines, often taking ten months or more merely to inform the lessee an application has been lodged. CLC complains to Aboriginal Affairs Minister Gerry Hand about the lack of progress.

MARCH

➤A report released by the Anti-Slavery Society established in the late 18th century in London concludes that the plight of Australian Aborigines has not improved much in 150 years.

➤The CLC and Warlpiri traditional landowners sign an agreement with North Flinders Mines to allow exploration on over 5,000 square kilometres of the Tanami Desert around The Granites. It is the first agreement negotiated from scratch under the Land Rights Act.

APRIL

➤Matters come to a head on excisions. Admitting 'disappointing' progress, Northern Territory Lands Department representatives agree to an 'action list' drawn up with CLC and DAA. Only one excision has been negotiated under the guidelines in Central Australia in three years of operation. It becomes clear to CLC that the Federal Government's Working Party is unlikely to achieve a just settlement for Aboriginal people awaiting living areas on pastoral properties.

➤Major flooding resurrects the Northern Territory Government campaign for a lake north of the Alice Springs Telegraph Station, but this time

1988 MARCH

They came from the North; they came from the West; they came from all points in between. More than 15,000 Anangu, Kooris, Murris, Noongars, Yapa and Yolgnu converged on Sydney in the days before 26 January 1988.

As white Australia celebrated a mere two-hundred years of clinging to the coast of the world's oldest land, black Australia and friends set out to mourn the effect of those two hundred years. But they also came together to celebrate an unbroken line of more than 40,000 years of cultural survival.

Over the days before the march, the trickle of people arriving in Sydney swelled to a flood. At La Perouse, heavy rain could not dampen the warmth of a joyful welcome at the arrival of the big convoy – buses, trucks and cars from Adelaide, Alice Springs, Darwin and Perth, complete with a police escort. Cheers, hugs and tears greeted the more than a thousand people who made the epic trip.

By the time 26 January came around, the atmosphere was electric. Thousands gathered at Redfern Park from early in the morning, making ready for the march. The red, yellow and black was everywhere.

Singers from Central Australia, bodies ochred, sat in a circle of spears to chant the songs of the desert. Alongside them, the white-painted, feather-decked men and women of the Top End broke into their own songs.

The dancers led off the march behind the chairmen of the Northern Territory Land Councils – Wenten Rubuntja and Galarrwuy Yunupingu. The streets of the city echoed with the clapping of boomerangs and shields, the click of the clapsticks, and drone of the didgeridu and the wailing chant of the songmen. Behind the dancers, Australia's biggest ever gathering of Aboriginal people walked in unity.

The march arrived at Belmore Park to a tumultuous welcome from supporters, who thronged the surrounding streets and cheered from the pedestrian overpass near Sydney's Central Station.

The march on to Hyde Park began as the crowd swelled to more than 40,000 people. Hyde Park south rapidly filled up as the march kept coming and coming.

Master of ceremonies Gary Foley, besieged with lost children messages early on, kept a good-humoured flow of patter up to the crowd as they waited for the speakers.

'Let's hope Bob Hawke and his Government get the message loud and clear from all these people here today,' he said. 'It's so magnificent to see black and white Australians here together in harmony. It's what we always said could happen. This is what Australia could and should be like.'

There was music – old and new – and dancing, speeches and more speeches and above all, a feeling of unity, solidarity and great happiness.

'Australia is too old to celebrate birthdays,' said Galarrwuy Yunupingu. 'It's about time we got together to wipe out the injustices of the past and develop a unity between black and white Australians which recognises Aboriginal people's commitment to our land.'

Land Rights News, March 1988

1988

the project is presented as a flood mitigation rather than a recreation lake. Chief Minister Steve Hatton blames the custodians who stopped the lake project for the deaths of three people during the floods.

Werlatye Atherre is now on the National Estate Register, but custodians are horrified to find new bulldozer trenches in the area. The CLC responds to requests from traditional custodians to organise meetings to discuss how to protect the site.

We are talking for the Aboriginal people and families of Alice Springs. We demand an apology from the Chief Minister Mr Steve Hatton for his statements since last week's flood. He said the flood should be blamed on Aboriginal people because we have not given permission for the dam because of our sacred sites. This is not true and he knows it...
The 1984 Board of Inquiry said that the Telegraph Station was not the right place for the dam and it wouldn't help stop a flood. What the government has done since then on flood mitigation has been four small things. We agreed with all of these, even though two of them went on our sacred sites. The Northern Territory Government has not been serious about flood mitigation. They keep talking about a recreation dam, but that won't stop the floods.
The real problem... is the new developments in town, such as the Ford Resort which causes flooding by blocking the overflow area from the Todd River into the boxwood swamp, and the Larapinta Valley and Mt John developments which cause big flows of water into the Todd River... Why has the Government allowed these new developments when we have warned them they make more trouble?
Statement by custodian meeting

➤The Prime Minister's wife Hazel Hawke opens the new museum of art and culture at Yuelamu (Mt Allan). The land claim over the area, which is an Aboriginal-owned cattle station, remains blocked because of Northern Territory Government litigation.

MAY

➤Mr Justice Howard Olney takes up his position as the new Aboriginal Land Commissioner.

JUNE

➤The Chairman of Telecom hands over a letter of 'permissive occupancy' for parts of the Barrow Creek Telegraph Station to the Kaytetye traditional landowners. Telecom's attempts to simply transfer title to the traditional landowners have been frustrated by the Northern Territory Government for the last two years. The CLC will assist the traditional owners to establish the Thangkenharenge Resource Centre and other facilities on the 4.5-hectare site.

1988

➢ CLC Chairman Wenten Rubuntja and NLC Chairman Galarrwuy Yunupingu present Prime Minister Bob Hawke with the Barunga Statement — a petition seeking government recognition of Aboriginal prior ownership of Australia and calling for a treaty. The Prime Minister agrees it is up to Aboriginal people to determine what should be in such a document.

Today there are lots of people living in this country. People who have come from all over the world. But we don't call them foreigners. We don't ask 'Where's your country? Where's your father from?' They have been born here. Their mother's blood is in this country. It doesn't matter if their father's father came from Indonesia or Japan or some other place. This is their country too now.
So all of us have to live together. We have to look after each other. We have to share this country.
And this means respecting each others laws and culture.
That's how it should be. We've all got to live like that. Teach each other and look after each other.
We have to work out a way of sharing this country, but there has to be an understanding of and respect of our culture, our law.
Hopefully that's what this Treaty will mean.
CLC Chairman Wenten Rubuntja

➢ In the Lake Amadeus land claim, Justice Michael Maurice finds against the majority of claimants represented by the CLC because the traditional land tenure principle relied upon by some claimants doesn't fit the model required by the Land Rights Act. Justice Maurice recommends that two small areas of land be granted. The recommended areas lie within Kings

BARUNGA

The Barunga Statement was presented to the Prime Minister of Australia, Bob Hawke, by the chairmen of the Central and Northern Land Councils, Wenten Rubuntja and Galarrwuy Yunupingu, on 12 June 1988, during the Barunga Sports and Cultural Festival.

The Statement takes the form of a petition set amidst a series of paintings. The words of the petition call for the Australian Government to recognise the rights of Australia's indigenous people while the paintings tell stories of the land – a reminder of where the words come from.

The design on the right was painted by Wenten Rubuntja, Lindsay Turner Jampijinpa and Dennis Williams Japanangka from Central Australia. It tells part of the Two-Women Dreaming which links together all the major language groups of the Centre and calls on Aboriginal people to come together to celebrate their culture and their country.

The three panels on the left were painted by artists from the NLC region and tell stories from the Crocodile Fire and Whale Dreamings which give their peoples title to the land and the sea.

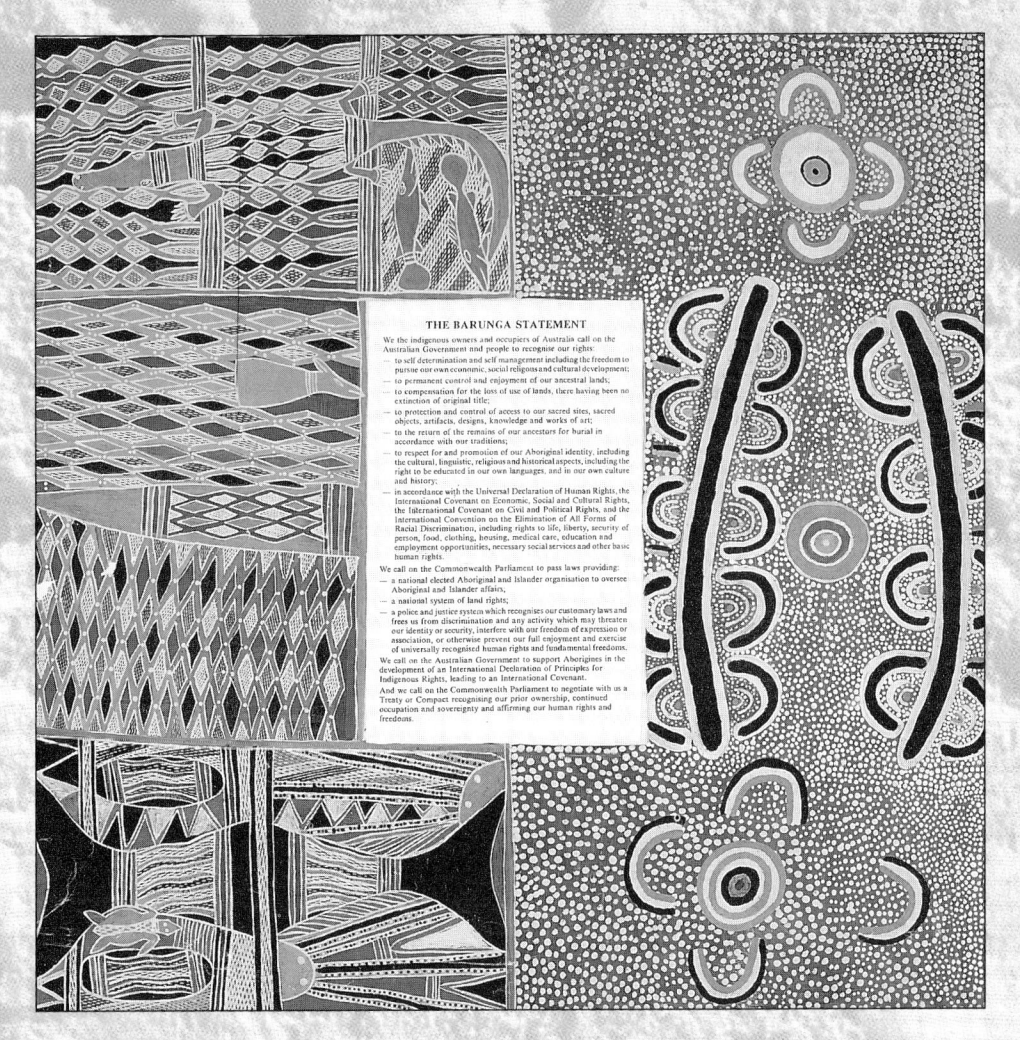

THE BARUNGA STATEMENT

We the indigenous owners and occupiers of Australia call on the Australian Government and people to recognise our rights:

- to self determination and self management including the freedom to pursue our own economic, social religious and cultural development;
- to permanent control and enjoyment of our ancestral lands;
- to compensation for the loss of use of lands, there having been no extinction of original title;
- to protection and control of access to our sacred sites, sacred objects, artifacts, designs, knowledge and works of art;
- to the return of the remains of our ancestors for burial in accordance with our traditions;
- to respect for and promotion of our Aboriginal identity, including the cultural, linguistic, religious and historical aspects, including the right to be educated in our own languages, and in our own culture and history;
- in accordance with the Universal Declaration of Human Rights, the International Covenant on Economic, Social and Cultural Rights, the International Covenant on Civil and Political Rights, and the International Convention on the Elimination of All Forms of Racial Discrimination, including rights to life, liberty, security of person, food, clothing, housing, medical care, education and employment opportunities, necessary social services and other basic human rights.

We call on the Commonwealth Parliament to pass laws providing:

- a national elected Aboriginal and Islander organisation to oversee Aboriginal and Islander affairs;
- a national system of land rights;
- a police and justice system which recognises our customary laws and frees us from discrimination and any activity which may threaten our identity or security, interfere with our freedom of expression or association, or otherwise prevent our full enjoyment and exercise of universally recognised human rights and fundamental freedoms.

We call on the Australian Government to support Aborigines in the development of an International Declaration of Principles for Indigenous Rights, leading to an International Covenant.

And we call on the Commonwealth Parliament to negotiate with us a Treaty or Compact recognising our prior ownership, continued occupation and sovereignty and affirming our human rights and freedom.

1988

Creek Station, which was leased to Ian Conway and Tim Lander after the land claim was lodged.

➤ Over the last twelve months, the Northern Territory Government gave consent to negotiate to applicants holding fifty-nine Exploration Lease Applications (ELAs) — double the number of the previous year — but the Government's assessment of the financial and technical capabilities of the 'miners' is inadequate and half the companies don't pursue their applications. On instruction from traditional owners, CLC engages in negotiations with six companies over thirteen ELAs.

JULY ➤ Angkerle Aboriginal Corporation purchases the Standley Chasm Kiosk, a successful tourist business operating on Aboriginal land near the chasm. The CLC assists Angkerle with legal advice and funding applications. The kiosk sells locally produced arts and crafts and employs several traditional owners, including a trainee manager and Angkerle plans to open a restaurant and an art gallery.

➤ Almost a decade after the Warumungu land claim was lodged, Land Commissioner Maurice recommends the grant of 6,400 square kilometres, but excludes a large area on the eastern side and two smaller areas because he isn't satisfied that traditional land ownership has been proved. Repeat claims are lodged and additional research begun.

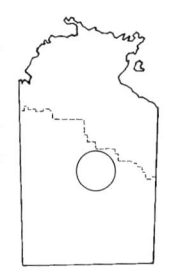

In his report, Maurice notes:

The country as a whole has profited, and continues to profit, from the dispossession of these people, and the use to which we put their lands. It is not simply a question of rectifying the wrongs of the past, as if the consequences of those wrongs had long ago been worked through: the simple truth is that they have not, yet as a nation we continue to enjoy the benefits from them.

AUGUST 23 ➤ The first resolution passed in the Commonwealth's new Parliament House is a recognition of Aboriginal people's prior ownership of Australia and their entitlement to self-management and self-determination. The resolution was drawn up by fourteen major churches.

The Queen, and the Senate and the House of Representatives of the Commonwealth of Australia acknowledge that:

Australia was occupied by Aboriginals and Torres Strait Islanders who had settled for thousands of years before British settlement at Sydney Cove on January 26, 1788;

1988

Aboriginals and Torres Strait Islanders suffered disposession and dispersal upon acquisition of their traditional lands by the British Crown;

Aboriginal and Torres Strait Islanders were denied full citizenship rights of the Commonwealth of Australia prior to May 27, 1967;

And affirm:

The importance of Aboriginal and Torres Strait Islander culture and heritage;

The entitlement of Aboriginals and Torres Strait Islanders to self-management and self-determination subject to the Constitution and the laws of the Commonwealth of Australia;

And consider it desirable that the Commonwealth further promote reconciliation with Aboriginal and Torres Strait Islander citizens providing recognition of their special place in the Commonwealth of Australia.

SEPTEMBER

➤ The United Nations' Working Group on Indigenous Populations says that Australian governments are in violation of international human rights obligations in their discriminatory treatment of Aboriginal and Islander people.

➤ In an attempt to resolve some of the detriment issues in the Warumungu land claim, CLC proposes a broad lease-back arrangement involving land adjoining the town boundaries to the Tennant Creek Town Council and the Northern Territory Government. The Government doesn't respond.

➤ The McLaren Creek land claim hearing starts at the station homestead.

OCTOBER

➤ Traditional owners receive title to the Yuelamu (Mt Allan) pastoral lease, nine years after the claim was lodged. It is the first land handed back in the CLC region for two years. Title was delayed three years by Northern Territory Government legal actions, and even after the handover the Northern Territory Government goes to the Federal Court to try and prevent the title being registered.

➤ The CLC and NLC's joint *Land Rights News* receives a special citation in the 1988 United Nations Media Peace Awards and the 1988 Print Newspaper Award of the Australian Human Rights Commission.

➤ The Northern Territory budget for drilling and equipping water supplies on excisions is slashed by more than half. It is only enough to provide water to three or four sites Territory-wide. CLC institutes a computer database of water resources and needs and plans to establish indepen-

1988

dent Central Australian Aboriginal Water Supply Units to give Aboriginal people skills and equipment to find and maintain their own supplies.

➤The Northern Territory Government introduces a Bill to replace the Aboriginal Sacred Sites Act with new legislation which would weaken Aboriginal control over the protection of sacred sites.

NOVEMBER ➤Mr Long Pwerle is elected as the new Chairman when the CLC meets at Harts Range. Mr Long is a Kaytetye man. His grandmother's country is Barrow Creek and his grandfather's country is Willowra. Mr Long lives at Alekarenge and already has a long history of involvement in Aboriginal organisations including the Central Land Council and the National Aboriginal Consultative Committee. Geoff Shaw is re-elected Deputy Chairman.

➤A Perth-based mining company, Frankenfeld Quarries applies to the Aboriginal Sacred Sites Protection Authority for clearance to mine the Devils Pebbles — an outcrop of granite boulders twelve kilometres north of Tennant Creek. The company wants to quarry granite for decorative tiles. When the authority consults the traditional landowners they refuse permission and apply for the sacred site to be registered.

DECEMBER ➤The Northern Territory Government's *Strehlow Research Centre Act* goes into effect. The Act, which was introduced without consulting Aboriginal people, controls the future of Aboriginal artefacts, sacred objects and other culturally important material collected by T.G.H. Strehlow, a renowned anthropologist who was born at Hermannsburg Mission and later worked as a patrol officer in Central Australia. There is no requirement for Aboriginal representation on the Board of Management or provision for the involvement of appropriate Aboriginal people in decisions about the collection. CLC asks the Commonwealth Government to withhold any financial assistance.

➤Atula Pastoral Lease is purchased by the Aboriginal Development Commission with CLC's assistance. A land claim is lodged over the property.

MT ALLAN

When Frankie Japanangka received the title papers from Aboriginal Affairs Minister Gerry Hand on 19 October 1988 the nine-year saga of the Mt Allan land claim should have been over – it wasn't. Within a week the Northern Territory Government was in the Federal Court in Sydney asking for the title to be declared invalid.

Aboriginal people bought the station in 1976 and lodged a land claim on behalf of the Anmatyerre and Warlpiri traditional landowners in 1979. The claim was heard by Mr Justice Kearney who found that traditional landowners had maintained strong traditional attachment to the land, performing regular ceremonies and rituals and instructing the young in traditional law. In his 1985 report he also noted that the station was well run.

The traditional landowners should have been given the paper title to their land that year but the handback was blocked by the Northern Territory Government which went to the Federal Court claiming that a disused stock route across the land claim was in fact a 'public road'. The Northern Territory Government's arguments were rejected there, so they took the matter to the High Court, which also knocked them back.

By the time of the title handover in 1988 the Northern Territory Government had wasted tens of thousands of dollars and three years of the traditional landowners' time – but they remained as litigious as ever.

This time they argued that a series of rough station tracks were public roads. The Federal Court turned down their arguments when it heard the case in 1989.

Then CLC Director Pat Dodson described the case as 'an extravagant waste of public money'.

> I estimate that more than $5 million has been spent running to court to stop the return of land to Aboriginal people,' said Mr Dodson, 'And they haven't won yet! The latest Mt Allan case involved five barristers, including two QCs spending four days in a Sydney court. Legal fees alone would be $40,000. Then there's the cost of flying witnesses down from Mt Allan and Darwin and of course all the preparatory work. All that in attempt to have ten dirt tracks declared public roads and cut out of the land grant.
>
> This Mt Allan case is only the latest and compared with the litigation costs in the Kenbi and Warumungu land claims, it's chickenfeed.
>
> Ever since the Land Rights Act came into force the Northern Territory Government has shamelessly fought tooth and nail trying to deny Aboriginal people land rights. They've raced off to court thirty times and are yet to win a case.
>
> Obviously the Government's political motivation is clouding their assessment of the legal issues, but of greater concern is the extravagant waste of public money.

The CLC Director challenged the Northern Territory Government to reveal how much money had been wasted in failed court challenges, but it refused to do so.

1989

JANUARY ➢ CLC opens a south-west regional office at Mutitjulu community near Uluru.

➢ Traditional landowners are shocked to find a front-end loader and other machinery at Kunjarra (Devils Pebbles), a registered sacred site near Tennant Creek. The Northern Territory Government has given a mining company approval to work on the area despite the opposition of custodians. When discussions with the mining company fail, traditional landowners obtain a court injunction to stop the work and maintain a protest camp for more than six weeks until the company retreats.

The Devils Pebbles/Kunjarra Munga Munga Dreaming is being threatened by the mining company. It is very sad to see our country being destroyed by taking our life on the land and just leaving the marks on our body and the song to sing and talk about, and nothing to look back where once our grandparents walked upon.
Christine Napanangka Plummer and Patrice Napurrula Frank

FEBRUARY ➢ The Northern Territory Government withdraws its proposed Aboriginal Areas Protection Bill for 'further consultation' following the protests of Aboriginal people throughout the Northern Territory. The Land Councils jointly draft 'minimum standards' for sacred sites protection. The cornerstone is the absolute right of Aboriginal custodians to control protection of sacred sites.

➢ The CLC reaches agreement with Otter Exploration N.L. to permit exploration over 3,091 square kilometres of the Tanami. The agreement includes sacred sites protection, opportunities for Aboriginal employment and compensation for traditional owners. Company representatives commend CLC for the 'excellent spirit' of the negotiations.

➢ The Northern Territory Government goes to the Federal Court to try and block the grant of land in the Lake Amadeus land claim. They want a declaration that the lease granted to Conway and Lander after the land claim was lodged is valid.

APRIL ➢ At a meeting called by the Northern Territory Power and Water Authority (PAWA), senior women custodians from four language groups conclusively reject the Alice Springs Telegraph Station dam proposal by demonstrating powerfully their continuing spiritual links with the site. PAWA promises to explore alternative sites upstream.

1989

➤ CLC enters into three exploration agreements with Tanami Joint Venture (TJV) covering 7,374 square kilometres of Aboriginal land. In addition to sacred site protection, compensation and employment opportunities, traditional landowners are also eligible to take up an equity interest in any mining venture that might ensue.

TJV, as operators of the Tanami mine, have established a very good relationship with the local Aboriginal people. This relationship and the constructive and positive approach adopted by the company contributed to the speed and success of negotiations.
These agreements are a further example of the capacity of traditional landowners to enter into commercial ventures and to contribute to the responsible economic development of the Northern Territory.
Mr Long Pwerle, CLC Chairman

➤ The first part of the Wakaya–Alyawarr land claim hearing begins. A last-minute settlement offer by Northern Territory Government is accepted by one group of traditional landowners but rejected by eight others who pursue the land claim. The offer provides for Northern Territory freehold title which is not as strong or secure as title under the Land Rights Act.

MAY

➤ The Aboriginal and Torres Strait Islanders Commission (ATSIC) Bill is introduced into Federal Parliament. It will dissolve DAA and establish elected regional Aboriginal councils and a national Aboriginal council to make decisions about policy and allocation of funds.

On the same day, Aboriginal Affairs Minister Hand says the Federal Government will legislate to provide living areas on Northern Territory pastoral leases because of the Northern Territory Government's inaction.

CLC Director Pat Dodson welcomes Mr Hand's announcement:

It is important that everyone is clear about how little land is being talked about. In Central Australia the average size of pastoral leases is about 3,000 square kilometres. The living areas that are needed average ten to fifteen square kilometres. No one is talking about the wholesale transfer of land.
Pat Dodson, CLC Director

➤ A Federal Court judge dismisses the Northern Territory Government appeal to block registration of the title to Mt Allan and orders the government to pay all costs. The Northern Territory Government appeals to the full bench of the Federal Court. The case is later settled out of court when the Government agrees to drop its legal action and pay the CLC's costs and traditional landowners agree to open two station roads to the public.

SACRED SITES PROTECTION

When the Aboriginal Land Rights Act was being drafted and redrafted by the Fraser Government in 1976 the CLC and other Aboriginal organisations opposed plans to give the Northern Territory Government power over sacred sites. The CLC argued that the Commonwealth Government should exercise its responsibility in this area and not hand those powers over to an administration that had repeatedly opposed Aboriginal rights; but the Land Councils lost that battle and in 1979 the Northern Territory's *Aboriginal Sacred Sites Act* came into effect.

Although the CLC was not satisfied with the legislation, the Aboriginal Sacred Sites Protection Authority (ASSPA) which it established, did enjoy a degree of independence from government control. The Authority spoke out against government projects like the proposed dam at Werlatye Atherre and eventually brought charges against then Lands Minister Marshall Perron over the desecration of a registered sacred site in 1984 (the prosecution did not proceed because of a legal loophole).

The Northern Territory Government however was also less than satisfied, and in October 1988 it introduced amendments designed to weaken sacred sites protection in line with the recommendations of the Martin Committee Report. The new legislation gave the Minister for Lands the power to overrule the new Aboriginal Areas Protection Authority (which would replace the ASSPA), have the final say on whether sacred sites should be protected or destroyed, and decide who should have access to sacred secret information.

When the Northern Territory Government refused to negotiate over the amendments the Central and Northern Land Councils launched a joint campaign for stronger sacred sites protection and the chairmen of the Central and Northern Land Councils made a joint statement:

> *This Bill is completely unacceptable and an insult to Aboriginal people. It will remove Aboriginal control of sacred site protection and give all power to the Northern Territory Government Minister.*
> *Aboriginal people have a right to protection of our sacred sites.*
> *We want the proposed law stopped. We want the Federal Government to make a stronger law and to help Aboriginal people to properly protect our sacred sites.*
> *The right to freedom of religion is enjoyed by all other Australians. Aboriginal people want the same right.*

Aboriginal people from Central Australia travelled in from the bush to set up a protest camp outside the Northern Territory Government offices in Alice Springs. At night there was dancing and ceremony, and by day leaflets were handed out to passers by and tourists, while hundreds of signatures were collected on a petition against the Bill.

Despite a number of amendments to the Bill the central problem with the new law remained: the Minister for Lands was given the final say on the protection or destruction of sacred sites. The CLC and NLC continued to push for Federal Government action to override the Northern Territory Government but without success.

On Friday 26 May the camp woke to the news that the Bill had passed through the Legislative Assembly in the early hours of the morning. The protestors were bitterly disappointed but decided to continue with the rally they had planned for Monday morning.

It was the biggest street demonstration Alice Springs had seen for many years as hundreds of people marched through town and rallied at the protest camp. Messages of support flowed in from across the country: from church congregations, trade unions, environment and peace groups, school children, politicians and interstate Aboriginal groups.

Rosie Furber spoke on behalf of the families of Mparntwe, whose traditional country is in and around Alice Springs:

> I'd like to say something about this new law the government is putting concerning our sacred sites. As my cousin said earlier on, we've been moved and we got no where to live now. Some of our people have got places to stop in the town camps, but we got nowhere to live.
> All our sacred sites have been taken away from us. In the olden days nobody was allowed to walk in our country here and now all the people are walking on our sacred grounds. We've got Dog Dreaming there, and we've got sacred tree here just near the Stuart Arms. And our dreaming trees on the east side, now there's a big water slide there. That's what development has done to our sacred sites around here.
> We've got a lookout on our sacred sites hill, that's Anzac Hill, and what now the Government's talking about is setting up a big hotel on Billy Goat Hill, that's our sacred sites too. So that's what has happened to our sacred sites, the only place we got left that nobody goes around now is Werlatye Atherre where the Government is talking about setting up a dam. And me and my family we don't want that dam there.
> Before the Northern Territory Government wanted to set up a recreation dam at our sacred site, that women's dreaming. And we fought with the Northern Territory Government through the old sacred sites law. But now with this new law being put through, they'll be able to do that now, put the dam there. And that would be a very sad thing for us to see the dam there.

1989

JUNE ➤ Five Arrernte families establish a protest camp alongside the Stuart Highway fifty kilometres north of Alice Springs to highlight their fourteen-year fight for living areas on Yambah Station.

We have set up the camp close to the highway to let the public know, and to let the Government here in the Territory know, that this is how we have been living for the past five years and we have had enough. We want it to stop.
We have had a lot of travellers from interstate, and from town, come in because they are curious. We tell them what is happening and show them how we are living and they have shown us support by signing our petition.
Margie Lynch, spokesperson for Mpweringe-Arnapipe Council

JULY ➤ Pat Dodson leaves CLC to return to his own country around Broome in Western Australia. He is appointed to the Royal Commission into Aboriginal Deaths in Custody. Kumantjayi Ross becomes CLC Director. Mr Ross, who was born and raised in Alice Springs, started work with the CLC in 1979 and is a business management graduate who had been Deputy Director since 1988.

➤ A University of Sydney report, commissioned by the CLC and other Alice Springs Aboriginal organisations, shows that Aboriginal wages, benefits and programs account for one-third of the Central Australian economy.

SEPTEMBER ➤ The Prime Minister and the Chief Minister sign a Memorandum of Agreement on excisions. Facing the threat of Commonwealth amendments to incorporate an excisions process in the Land Rights Act the

THE YAMBAH MOB

In June 1989 five Arrernte families set up a protest camp alongside the Stuart Highway forty-five kilometres north of Alice Springs. The families, who were known as the Yambah mob, had been fighting for fourteen years for title to their traditional land, and they resolved to stay put until they got justice.

The CLC began negotiations on behalf of the Lynch, McMillan, Palmer, Rice and Turner families in 1975 and in the early 1980s lodged land claims on nearby stock routes and reserves. The families formed the Mpweringe-Arnpipe Council in 1984 and moved out of Alice Springs to set up camps on a stock route and reserve near Yambah Station and demonstrate their commitment to their traditional country. Because they had no 'legal' land title, government departments refused to provide even the most basic services, and even drinking water had to be carted by truck from Alice Springs and stored in recycled forty-four-gallon fuel drums.

They resisted intimidation and gunshots, but after five years of patience they decided it was time to increase the pressure with a visible protest camp. Over forty people moved into the roadside camp, living in canvas tents and donated tin sheds with an old minibus serving as a classroom for the children.

The story of the Yambah mob and their fight for living areas and excisions helped to focus national attention on 'the people that land rights forgot' – the people who were forced off their country by the pastoral industry.

We have done everything asked of us under whitefella law to try to get a small part of our land back,' said Magdalene Lynch.

'Our fathers, mothers, grandmothers and grandfathers built up these cattle stations. But the greed of the pastoralists, the pigheadedness of the Northern Territory Government, and the failure of the Federal Government to provide for us as directed by white Australia in the 1967 referendum, has led us to despair and now to direct action.'

The Yambah protest camp built political pressure for the Memorandum of Agreement between the Federal and Territory Governments and as part of that agreement the families were promised title to forty-three square kilometres at Black Tank Bore on the Sandover Stock Route and three small areas on the North–South Stock Route at Yambah.

1989

Northern Territory agrees to amend the Crown Lands Act so that Aboriginal people can apply for excisions from pastoral leases. The Commonwealth agrees to hand back title to some stock routes and reserves to Aboriginal claimants. The hope is that the two processes will be enough to meet the land needs of 'the people that land rights forgot' – people whose traditional land has been taken by the pastoral industry.

The Northern Territory Government agrees to establish a tribunal to arbitrate on applications refused by the Minister for Lands, but the land councils are not consulted on the agreement and the compromise doesn't recognise applications based on traditional ownership.

OCTOBER ➢ The *Miscellaneous Act Amendment (Aboriginal Community Living Areas) Act* passes through the Northern Territory Legislative Assembly. The Act is supposed to provide a framework for excisions but does not live up to the terms agreed between the Commonwealth and Northern Territory Governments in the Memorandum of Agreement. The CLC is particularly concerned at the long waiting periods written into the application procedure.

NOVEMBER ➢ The Central Land Council meeting at Arrawajin, south-east of Tennant Creek, affirms its opposition to the Northern Territory Aboriginal Sacred Sites Act and calls on the Commonwealth Government to take action to protect sacred sites under the Land Rights Act in a unanimous resolution:

As custodians of Aboriginal Sacred Sites we know Aboriginal Law does not change. We will not let changes to whitefella law allow the possible deliberate destruction of our sites.
All custodians of Aboriginal Sacred Sites will keep on standing strong to protect our Sacred Sites as our people have for more than 40,000 years.

➢ The CLC Chairman Mr Long Pwerle calls on the Commonwealth Government to withhold Commonwealth funding from the proposed Strehlow Research Centre which will house the Strehlow collection of sacred objects, artefacts, films and anthropological information. The Northern Territory Government has already passed an Act to establish the research and tourist centre without consulting Aboriginal people.

The Act has to be changed to make sure that appropriate Aboriginal people control the collection, and that the traditional custodians are able to decide what happens to their property.
If some custodians want their objects back then they should be given back, but according to the Strehlow Act it is illegal to give anything back.
Long Pwerle, CLC Chairman

1989

➢ The *Aboriginal and Torres Strait Islanders Commission (ATSIC) Act* is passed. The Act provides a national elected representative structure for Commonwealth Aboriginal Affairs. It is one of the most amended pieces of legislation in the history of the Commonwealth Parliament and is passed despite the strenuous objections of the Northern Territory Government.

➢ In the Lake Amadeus land claim, the Federal Court declares the 'lease' of Kings Creek Station invalid because the land already had been claimed under the Land Rights Act. The decision is a significant victory and has flow-on effects to other land claims, but the after effects of the 'lease' are complicated. The lessees sue the Northern Territory Government for compensation but refuse to deal with the CLC. Their investment at Kings Creek becomes a major stumbling block to the land being handed back to traditional landowners.

DECEMBER

➢ The *Aboriginal Land Rights (Northern Territory) Amendment Act 1989* is passed, adding twenty-six portions of stock routes and stock reserves in the CLC area to Schedule I of the Land Rights Act. As the scheduled areas are handed back and become Aboriginal land, traditional landowners withdraw their claims on other stock routes and reserves. This concludes the long-running dispute with the Northern Territory Government and the Northern Territory Cattlemen's Association over stock route land claims.

In November 1989 Don Lynch spoke to *Land Rights News:*

Before Kidman got that country, we had that land. The land was there all the time. They put their mark around the boundary – that's whitefella way. When they put that line they cut our country in half. But we had our map all the time since the earth was put up. The Aboriginal map is different than squares. It's just like a snake, not square. Between tree and tree, hill and hill, that's how we follow our story. All the country's named. Just like when the white man dug out and named the bore – Ironwood Bore, Snake Well, Top Bore and all them. But all of them have got Aboriginal names, different names.

Today you see one hill there and 'No you can't go across, that's the boundary!' They got surveyor's pegs there. 'No you can't go there that's the station, you might get shot.'

'What I want now is to get a bit of land for my kids while I'm still alive. We're entitled to our land.

We're entitled to that land, because it's my father's and grandfather's land, it belongs to us. We only want a small bit, an excision.

That station owner, his father used to visit the camps and play with the kids when he was young. We grew him up. He was eating goanna, sugar ants and everything with us. We taught him Arrernte language.

1989

In 1984 we moved back up to Yambah and set up camp on that stock route. At first we thought we'd stay a few months camping then we'd get a proper place, but we're still waiting, more than five years now. It's been a hard time. We've had to pay ourselves to get water trucked up from town.

That young fella [the station owner] tried to put us over in the corner on the western side, but that's different country for different Aboriginals. That doesn't belong to us.

Now we're going to get that stock route [Black Tank Bore] but we still want to talk about an excision. There's only three old blokes left holding that country now. That stock routes all right but I still want to get an excision over on the eastern side at Alparla, near the Bond Springs boundary. That's still the place I want – my country.

1990

JANUARY

➢ The CLC establishes a north-west regional office at Kalkarindji, near Daguragu.

➢ The new Aboriginal Areas Protection Authority (AAPA) issues a work certificate authorising the Northern Territory Government's proposed flood mitigation dam on the Todd River at Junction Waterhole, nine kilometres north of Alice Springs. The Junction Waterhole dam will damage and desecrate known sacred sites, including one which will be permanently submerged under water. Many of the initial consultations have been conducted by Northern Territory Government ministers and staff from the Department of Mines and Energy rather than the AAPA. Not only have many traditional landowners been left out of discussions but a lot of confusion has been created about the basic facts of the proposal — one tour of the dam site took traditional landowners to a site two kilometres away.

Junction Waterhole in 1990, the site of the proposed Alice Springs dam.

BARROW CREEK WARRIORS

In 1874 ninety Kaytetye people were killed by state troopers in retaliation for the killing of two linesmen at Barrow Creek Telegraph Station.

The reasons for the conflict are not clear. Some say the dispute was over women, others that the conflict erupted when the linesmen fenced off an important waterhole and refused the Kaytetye access to water and rations during a time of drought.

A hundred years after the Barrow Creek massacre the Kaytetye people began a new fight for control of the Barrow Creek Telegraph Station.

'This should be the Territory's first Aboriginal war memorial,' said Kaytetye woman Barbara Shaw. 'Our people died defending their right to protect their land.'

The handover should have been straightforward. Telecom owned title to the whole Telegraph Station area and wanted to transfer title for the historic buildings to the Conservation Commission of the Northern Territory (CCNT) with the remaining land and building going to the Kaytetye people's Thangkenharenge Aboriginal Corporation. In 1986 an in-principle agreement for the transfer was reached between the parties but then the problems began.

The Northern Territory Government argued that the whole area should be transferred to the CCNT. They raised all sorts of objections to the subdivision to try and limit or prevent the transfer, but after four years of negotiations, title was finally handed over in February 1990.

Thangkenharenge now runs a community resource centre from the site and is conducting research to gather material for an Aboriginal museum that will tell the story of the Kaytetye and their struggle.

Speaking at the opening of the resource centre, CLC Deputy Chairman Geoffrey Shaw talked about the importance of Kaytetye history:

> We've been through two massacres and we're still here. We've been scattered to the four winds, but remember: you are not just someone living in a street or town somewhere. You are Kaytetye people!

1990

FEBRUARY

➤Senior women custodians for Kunjarra (Devils Pebbles) complain to police about harassment by a mining developer, Lutz Frankenfeld, who wants permission to quarry granite from Kunjarra. The custodians refused permission to mine the area when Mr Frankenfelds's company applied to the former Aboriginal Sacred Sites Protection Authority in November 1988, and now he visits senior custodians at their homes claiming to have been encouraged to approach them directly by a Northern Territory Government minister. The harassment highlights the problems of the amended Aboriginal Sacred Sites Act under which the Minister for Lands can release confidential information including the names of custodians.

He was talking sweet to us. Talking about royalties for our sacred sites. I told him I'm sorry he cannot have that sacred site and I showed him other stones he can have that are not sacred.
Topsy Nelson Napurrula

➤When the CLC attempts to clarify the procedures for excision applications under the Northern Territory Government's new legislation, the Minister for Lands informs the CLC that there are no administrative guidelines. Although many pastoral living area applications under Northern Territory legislation date back nearly fifteen years, more than 130 current applications must now start from scratch. The CLC attempts to begin direct negotiations with pastoralists, but most refuse to participate on the advice of the Northern Territory Cattlemen's Association.

➤Aboriginal Affairs Minister Gerry Hand hands over title to 2,641 square kilometres of land, the Chilla Well land claim, north-west of Alice Springs. This is the first area handed back in the CLC region since Mt Allan in October 1988.

MARCH

➤The ALP is returned to government, although by a much slimmer margin. The CLP campaign in the Territory focussed on Aboriginal issues but local Labor member Warren Snowdon is returned to office with an increased vote – the only swing towards Labor anywhere in Australia. The Land Councils renew their call for consultations on a treaty.

ALICE SPRINGS DAM PART 2: JUNCTION WATERHOLE

After ten years of failing to convince the traditional landowners to allow the destruction of Werlatye Atherre, the Northern Territory Government examined other locations for a dam. Junction Waterhole was the first choice and in 1989 the Northern Territory Government began to examine the engineering and consult traditional landowners.

In January 1990 the AAPA issued a certificate under the Aboriginal Sacred Sites Protection Act authorising a dam to be built at Junction Waterhole. It was the second certificate issued. The first had authorised a dry flood mitigation dam but the January certificate authorised a dam half-full of water — a fact that led many to believe that the proposal was really a disguised recreation lake.

Chief Minister Marshall Perron announced the dam proposal and released a Draft Environmental Impact Statement (draft EIS) and scale model for public comment in June. He told the media that the traditional landowners had agreed to the proposal following 'impeccable' consultations.

The traditional landowners were horrified: many had not been consulted at all and others had only been given half the story. None had the chance to seek expert advice or examine the detailed proposal and model now on display.

The CLC engaged an expert dam engineer, Dr Stephen Webb, to review the proposal presented in the Draft EIS. He found that the dam was more like a recreation lake than a flood mitigation structure, and said the proposal was poorly designed, would do little towards saving lives and could not be built under the conditions of the AAPA Certificate.

The CLC lodged a submission on the Draft EIS with the Northern Territory Government stating that the Government had ignored some traditional landowners and misled others during consultation. The Northern Territory Government dismissed these objections and gave approval for the dam to proceed.

In January 1991 preliminary work began and the CLC applied to the Minister for Aboriginal Affairs, Robert Tickner, to stop the project under the Aboriginal and Torres Strait Islander Heritage Protection Act. Mr Tickner held discussions with Northern Territory Government ministers while work continued. In March traditional landowners found that sacred sites were already being damaged, and under pressure from the Commonwealth, the Northern Territory Government called a temporary halt to work. A meeting was held between officials from both governments and the CLC on 25 March 1991, and the CLC was able to demonstrate the inadequacy of the consultations. All parties — including the Northern Territory Government officers — agreed on the need for work to stop for further consultations with traditional landowners, but the Chief Minister refused to accept the advice of his staff and ordered work to resume. Late that night Mr Tickner issued a declaration to protect the sacred sites through a temporary halt to work so that traditional landowners could be consulted.

Over 100 traditional landowners met with representatives from the Chief Minister's office, ATSIC, AAPA and the CLC to discuss the dam. Angry at the lack of consultation and the damage already done the traditional landowners rejected the proposal. A few days later the AAPA withdrew its certificate and the Northern Territory Government announced that it would redesign the dam and seek permission for a revised proposal in the same area.

A month later the Northern Territory Power and Water Authority (PAWA) lodged an application with the AAPA to build a similar dam in the same location. The design would still damage and destroy a number of important sites but had been modified to hold less water. In the words of one traditional landowners it was 'just the old dam with a hole in it'.

PAWA and AAPA organised a series of meetings to consult the traditional landowners but the answer was always the same: they would not approve any proposal that desecrated and damaged sites.

In October the AAPA advised PAWA that it would not issue a certificate to authorise work. At the direction of the Minister responsible for the Aboriginal Areas Protection Authority, Max Ortmann, the Authority reviewed its decision but in January 1992 advised him that it could not issue a certificate.

Under the 1989 amendments to the Aboriginal Sacred Sites Act the Minister had been given the power to override the decision of the AAPA and issue a certificate without the Authority's approval and on the 4 March Mr Ortmann announced that he would do just that.

At the request of the traditional landowners the CLC arranged a meeting with Mr Ortmann and Aboriginal Affairs Minister Robert Tickner but the discussion was cut short when Mr Ortmann abused traditional landowners and stormed out. The CLC applied to Mr Tickner for a declaration to protect the sacred sites under threat and on 16 March he issued a declaration for a thirty-day halt to work. He later extended this to sixty days and appointed Mr Hal Wootten QC to conduct an inquiry into whether he should make a permanent order to protect the sites.

Mr Wootten received submissions from the CLC, the Northern Territory Government and other interested parties before delivering his report and recommendations to Mr Tickner.

On 16 May 1992 Mr Tickner issued a declaration under s.10 of the Aboriginal and Torres Strait Islanders Heritage Protection Act to protect the sacred sites around Junction Waterhole for a period of twenty years, effectively preventing the construction of the proposed dam. It was only the second s.10 declaration ever made and was a major victory for the Arrernte traditional landowners who had fought for so long.

1990

APRIL ➢ Robert Tickner is appointed as the new Minister for Aboriginal Affairs.

➢ The CLC signs a new exploration agreement with North Flinders Mines at Lajamanu. The agreement reached between traditional landowners and the company covers 138 square kilometres adjoining the existing Granites Gold Mine.

➢ CLC enters into an agreement with Magellan Petroleum for exploration over 15,859 square kilometres in the Ngalia Basin, which extends from west of Nyirrpi through Yuendumu towards the Stuart Highway. About half of the area to be explored is on Aboriginal land and this is the first oil and gas exploration permit issued in the CLC area since the 1987 amendments to the Land Rights Act.

In that time the CLC has negotiated mining company access to 35,000 square kilometres of Aboriginal land. Ninety-four exploration applications have been received and eighty per cent of these have been processed. Ninety-five per cent of the Northern Territory's mineral output by value comes from Aboriginal land.

MAY ➢ Aboriginal Land Commissioner Olney recommends that only part of the Wakaya–Alyawarr land claim be handed back after ruling that some traditional landowners are unable to fit the criteria in the Land Rights Act. The decision is a major disappointment to the traditional landowners, since it means a large area, which includes the Canteen Creek community, is not recommended for grant.

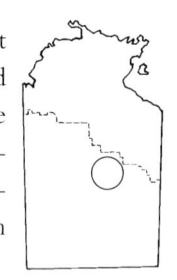

JUNE ➢ The Power and Water Authority releases a 280-page draft Environmental Impact Statement for the 'Proposed Flood Mitigation and Recreation Dam' at Junction Waterhole. It's the first public information released on the dam and many custodians are shocked and angry. They reject claims that they approved the project and approach the CLC for help. The Land Council employs a dam engineer, Dr Stephen Webb, to evaluate the project.

1990

➢ A CLC delegation joins indigenous representatives from around the world at the United Nations Working Group on Indigenous Populations (WGIP) in Geneva, and the World Council of Indigenous Peoples and the International Indigenous Women's Conference in Norway. The WGIP meets annually to work towards an international standard for the protection of indigenous rights.

When I went to Norway and Tromsø these two ladies took me to their house for a cup of tea and they were asking me lots of questions. They belong to that place, and I was telling them we've got to show something to our children, so our children can grow up really strong. So they can look out on their own country and their own sacred sites.
We got to do that. We got to fight for our children and our land, and we got to put our children to carry on. And they were really pleased.
Topsy Nelson Napurrula, CLC delegate to the World Council for Indigenous Peoples, 1990

JULY

➢ The National Federation of Land Councils calls on the Federal Government to honour its promise of a treaty with Aboriginal people, rejecting a proposed 'instrument of reconciliation'.

AUGUST

➢ One of Australia's leading dam engineers, Dr Stephen Webb, tells custodians that the proposed dam at Junction Waterhole is poorly designed and unsuitable for flood mitigation. Dr Webb was engaged by the CLC to provide custodians with an independent assessment of the dam proposal. Custodians reiterate their opposition to the dam but Northern Territory Government officials, including the Chief Minister, Marshall Perron, claim they have already given their approval.

CLC Director Kumanjayi Ross says that the mishandling of the dam highlights the failure of the new sacred sites legislation:

They've been playing this dam every which way. They told the non-Aboriginal people that they had the sacred sites clearance to build this dam. That's a lie.
They told Aboriginal people that they were proposing a flood mitigation dam that would save lives. That's a lie.

SACRED OBJECTS

In 1990 the CLC arranged for the return of almost a hundred secret and sacred objects from the South Australian Museum to their rightful owners in Central Australian communities. The return included objects that had been sold to the Museum by Professor Ted Strehlow.

The control of sacred material has been a major issue for the CLC since the council was formed. Early delegations to lobby governments over land rights legislation also took the opportunity to visit museums and other institutions to discuss the return of sacred objects.

The 1976 delegation which helped shape the Aboriginal Land Rights Act carried a *tjuringa* – a sacred object — which was shown to Prime Minister Malcolm Fraser as a symbol of the delegation's authority. The delegation also visited museums in Adelaide, Melbourne and Sydney and attempted to meet Professor Ted Strehlow, whose collection of sacred objects is regarded as the most important in Australia.

Professor Strehlow, who was born at Hermannsburg and who collected most of his material in Central Australia, refused to meet the delegation or to consider that 'his' objects might ever be returned to the rightful owners. The bulk of Professor Strehlow's collection is now held by the Strehlow Research Centre in Alice Springs and is controlled by legislation which prevents custodians from ever being able to reclaim their material.

Professor Strehlow and his supporters argued that Aboriginal custodians don't want the objects returned or that returning the material is 'too dangerous', but the traditional owners have consistently maintained that the future of these objects must be determined by the rightful owners.

Determining who the right people are requires careful research and consultation to identify the custodians and to determine what they want to do with their objects – that means giving the custodians the right to have their objects held in a museum or other institution for safekeeping or to hold it themselves. Experience has shown that when that process occurs many custodians do want to take control of their own sacred objects which they regard as representing not only their land and dreamings and culture but also part of their own selves.

Following the CLC's 1976 delegation, *Central Australian Land Rights News* reported, 'It looks like it will be a hard job to get *churingas* back.' It was an accurate assessment, but more and more museums, and even individuals with single objects or small collections, are now approaching the CLC to try and get these objects back to their rightful owners.

1990

And they told everyone that this full dam proposal was the best way to solve the town's flood problem. Well, now that we've had an independent expert examine the proposal we all know that this dam is a waste of money that would never do the job.
Kumanjayi Ross, CLC Director

➤The Aboriginal Rabbit Control Program is established at Mutitjulu and Imanpa communities to reduce the feral population, provide meat for community stores and employment for community members.

SEPTEMBER

➤Chief Minister Marshall Perron calls on the Commonwealth Government to transfer control of the Land Rights Act to the Northern Territory Government. He wants to end land claims, remove the traditional landowner's right to consent to mining, weaken sacred sites protection, reduce funding for the Land Councils, and the break-up of the Land Councils into smaller groups.

Speaking on behalf of Aboriginal people throughout Central Australia we say that land rights must stay with the Commonwealth Government because the Northern Territory Government has fought against land rights for many years and is not trusted by Aboriginal people.
CLC resolution, Negri River 17 October 1990

➤Centrecorp signs a joint venture agreement for a $17-million wilderness lodge at Watarrka (Kings Canyon) National Park. The resort is to include a three-star 100-room lodge, 160 backpacker beds, and extensive caravan and camping grounds.

We want to be part of everything that happens in the Northern Territory – the whole growth of this place. We want to be able to benefit from what happens in the Northern Territory because besides you people it belongs to us also, and the rest of Australia.
CLC Deputy Chairman Geoff Shaw

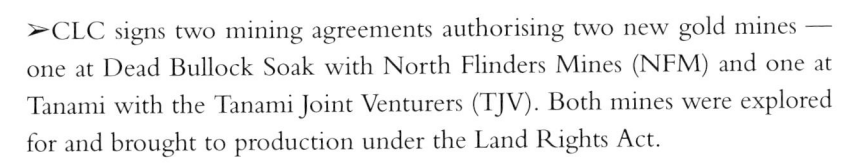

➤CLC signs two mining agreements authorising two new gold mines — one at Dead Bullock Soak with North Flinders Mines (NFM) and one at Tanami with the Tanami Joint Venturers (TJV). Both mines were explored for and brought to production under the Land Rights Act.

This project has moved smoothly and quickly from exploration to production under the provisions of the Land Rights Act. TJV has built a

1990

strong and positive relationship with Aboriginal people and their representatives in the CLC that has been of benefit to us all.
Mike Palmer, TJV General Manager

OCTOBER ➤Northern Territory Freehold Title for Gosse Bluff Scientific Reserve is granted to members of Tnorula Aboriginal Corporation, which represents the traditional landowners. The corporation then leases the area back to the Conservation Commission of the Northern Territory for a period of ninety-nine years. The grant follows years of disappointment and negotiation following the secret alienation of the area in 1984, which prevented traditional owners from claiming the land under the Land Rights Act. A local management committee with four traditional owners and two CCNT representatives is proposed to advise on day-to-day management.

➤The first applications for community living areas are lodged by the CLC under the Crown Lands Act which the Northern Territory Government amended following the Memorandum of Agreement on living areas. Sixteen applications will be lodged over the next eighteen months but only four pastoralists are willing to negotiate.

NOVEMBER ➤ATSIC Regional Council elections are held throughout Australia. CLC Deputy Chair Geoff Shaw is elected Commissioner for the Central Australian Zone and Chairman of the Alice Springs ATSIC Regional Council.

1991

JANUARY

➢ The Northern Territory Government releases the Final Environmental Impact Statement on the Junction Waterhole dam. The report says that custodians have been consulted by the Aboriginal Areas Protection Authority (AAPA) and given approval for sites to be destroyed. The objections of custodians, which have been made publicly and in submissions to the Government since the project was announced, are ignored. CLC seeks a declaration from the Minister for Aboriginal Affairs, Robert Tickner, to protect the sites under the *Aboriginal and Torres Strait Islanders Heritage Protection Act*. Northern Territory Chief Minister Marshall Perron tells Alice Springs residents that work on the dam will commence in May.

FEBRUARY

➢ After two years of intensive hearings and investigations the Royal Commission into Aboriginal Deaths in Custody releases its National Report. The report contains 339 recommendations in five volumes and addresses underlying issues including the dispossession of Aboriginal land and culture, and Aboriginal exclusion from economic benefits. The Commission supports the granting of Aboriginal land rights Australia-wide and Aboriginal people's right to control access and development of their land.

The Aboriginal Land Rights (Northern Territory) Act 1976 *is regarded by Aboriginal people as the benchmark of achievable land rights legislation.*
[Aboriginal people] are united in their view that land... is the key to their cultural and economic survival as a people.
Royal Commission into Deaths in Custody National Report, 19.1.1, 19.2.6

➢ The CLC meeting at Wanmara, near Kings Canyon, unanimously opposes moves by the Northern Territory Government to wrest control of the Land Rights Act from the Commonwealth Government.

MARCH

➢ When custodians are grudgingly allowed to visit the Alice Springs dam construction site, they discover earthworks under way and sacred sites already damaged or threatened. They establish a protest camp outside the gates to the construction area.

Under pressure from the Commonwealth, Chief Minister Marshall Perron stops work on the dam for a few days to allow talks between the parties. On 25 March representatives from the CLC, the AAPA, Commonwealth and Northern Territory Governments meet in Alice Springs and agree that work should not resume until there are further consultations with custodians. That night Chief Minister Marshall Perron overturns the decision of his officers and orders the bulldozers back in. At

1991

The damaged area of Junction Waterhole.

midnight Aboriginal Affairs Minister Tickner issues a declaration under s.9 of the *Aboriginal and Torres Strait Islanders Heritage Protection Act* to protect the sacred sites.

APRIL ➤Aboriginal Affairs Minister Robert Tickner, attends the CLC meeting at Intjartnama, ninety kilometres west of Alice Springs, to discuss the Commonwealth Government's proposal for a council of reconciliation. Delegates express concern about the long wait through the decade-long process but support greater recognition of Aboriginal rights and culture, and give unanimous support to the process. Tickner returns to Canberra with the CLC's support and a handful of dirt from Intjartnama. Cabinet decides to back the process of reconciliation that night.

➤A meeting of over one hundred custodians rejects the Junction Waterhole dam proposal and decries the damage to sites which has already occurred. The AAPA is forced to revoke the certificate but Chief Minister Marshall Perron says that the dam will be redesigned and another proposal presented.

Protestors and the press at the gates of the proposed dam site.

➤Title to two small areas of land at Honeymoon Bore and Sandover River are handed back to Alyawarr traditional landowners, the first of twenty-six portions of stock routes and stock reserves in the CLC region to be handed back under the 1989 amendments to the Land Rights Act. Both

98

1991

areas were subject to long and bitter negotiations for excisions, which kept traditional owners living for many years in car bodies and makeshift shelters without even basic services.

➤The Yurrkuru (Brookes Soak) land claim hearing begins near the site where Brookes was killed in 1928. The small area under claim is of great historical as well as cultural importance to the traditional landowners because of its association with the Coniston Massacre.

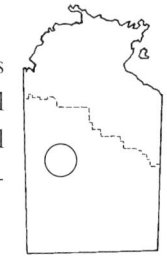

MAY

➤The Northern Territory Government introduces amendments to the Crown Lands Act prohibiting excisions within two kilometres of a homestead. The Northern Territory Government backdates the law to March 1990 so that some existing applications are retrospectively outlawed. The CLC protests to the Northern Territory and the Federal Governments, but the law is passed.

➤Title to 2,852 square kilometres of the Warumungu land claim area is handed back to traditional owners. It is the first part of the Warumungu land to be returned but represents less than half of the area recommended for grant. The handback is made possible by the Northern Territory Government's acceptance — finally — of a compromise offer on land near the town. The traditional owners agree to give substantial areas of land around Tennant Creek to the Northern Territory Government in return for title to two areas of land outside the claim area which contain important sacred sites.

➤AAPA receives an application for a certificate allowing construction of a re-designed flood mitigation dam at Junction Waterhole. The new proposal will still destroy and desecrate sacred sites.

JUNE

➤The CLC signs a new mineral exploration agreement with the Tanami Joint Venturers. The agreement covers 3,561 square kilometres of land around Mt Winnecke, between Tanami and Lajamanu.

➤The Council for Aboriginal Reconciliation Bill is passed to establish a mechanism for discussion of the reconciliation of Aboriginal and non-

1991

Aboriginal Australians. Former CLC Director Pat Dodson is appointed Council Chairman and former CLC Chairman Wenten Rubuntja becomes a member of the Reconciliation Council.

➢ The Strehlow Research Centre is opened in Alice Springs. Despite CLC objections, the ATSIC Commissioners approve the grant of $1.5 million to the Northern Territory Government toward the cost of construction.

I don't think Strehlow would have liked this museum. My grandfather taught him all about objects and ceremonies. We need those things. We need them for ceremony and schooling our younger generation. And after, when they learn, they can school their young ones. All Aborigines need them things to be put in our sacred sites and not in a museum. To use it and put them where they used to be.
When I feel lonely I just start singing my songs that my Grandpa taught me and I'm happy, but objects are always on my mind. We've got strong law. Whitefella laws are weak. They change the papers around. We don't change the paper. We've got it in our mind, in our caves — there's a whole book lying there.
What are we going to do if we don't get those objects? What's going to happen?
The old people and the old people after me, they'll be lost like an old mob of sheep just roaming around the country with nothing, nothing to show their kids.
Max Stuart, CLC Executive Member

➢ The remains of Cubadgee, a Warumungu man whose bones had been held in the South Australian Museum, are returned to Tennant Creek and buried by his family. It is the first such burial in Australia.

You're back home now. This is your home. You've been gone from here — now you've come back and you're resting in your own land.
The whole family came up to you, so you can rest in peace in your own land.
Brian Tennyson speaking at Cubadgee's graveside

JULY ➢ The Anindilyakwa Land Council is formed to represent the traditional landowners of Groote and Bickerton islands. These islands had been part of the Northern Land Council region but Aboriginal Affairs Minister Robert Tickner decided to establish a separate land council following a plebiscite.

➢ Mistake Creek pastoral lease in the north-west corner of the CLC region is purchased on behalf of the Tjupanyin Aboriginal Corporation. Traditional landowners lodge a claim over the property which they con-

CUBADGEE

In June 1991, the remains of Dick Cubadgee were returned to his descendants and buried near Tennant Creek. Cubadgee was a young Warumungu man, who acted as a guide, interpreter and go-between for explorer Dick Lindsay in the 1880s. His skills, in negotiating with different groups throughout Central Australia smoothed the way for Lindsay and earned the explorer's respect and admiration.

In 1887, 1888 and 1889 Lindsay took Cubadgee south, to the Royal Geographical Societies and International Exhibitions in Adelaide and Melbourne, and to Adelaide's Government House. Little was known about Aboriginal culture and the outback then, but there was a lot of public interest and Cubadgee's charismatic personality, and his displays of boomerang throwing and fire-lighting, made him an exotic attraction.

In 1889 Cubadgee and Lindsay returned to Central Australia, but during the expedition Cubadgee became sick with a cancerous tumour on his neck. Lindsay sent him to the Royal Adelaide Hospital to have the tumour removed, and although the operation appears to have been successful, Cubadgee contracted tuberculosis while in hospital.

Cubadgee had made many friends during his long sickness. Nurses and members of the Women's Auxiliary read him stories from the Bible, and in return he told them stories of Warumungu culture and life in the bush. As he became increasingly ill, he began to talk with greater and greater emphasis of the importance of the land to Aboriginal people and of the damage Europeans were doing. According to records of the South Australian Museum, he told hospital staff that 'the whites were intruders in his country and should leave his people alone'. He asked to be allowed to return to his country, but was kept in hospital.

Cubadgee died on 15 September, 1889. He was just nineteen years old.

To this point Cubadgee's life had been quite unusual, but after his death, he suffered a fate shared by thousands of Aboriginal people over the years – his remains were placed in a museum.

Cubadgee had to wait over one hundred years before he could rest back in his own country, but when he came back he was warmly welcomed by his family.

'It's an important thing, because he went away from here, this is his traditional place, this is his dreaming country, which is his father's country', said Jimmy Frank, who shares the Jurnkurakurr Dreaming with Cubadgee.

As another Warumungu man put it: 'See that rock there, that's his body, see that tree there, that's his body.'

1991

tinue to operate with more than 10,000 head of stock under Aboriginal management.

➢ Custodians for the Junction Waterhole area tell the Aboriginal Areas Protection Authority and Northern Territory Government representatives that they will not approve any proposal for a dam at Junction Waterhole that damages and desecrates sacred sites. They maintain their position at a series of meetings over the next two months.

➢ Justice Peter Gray of the Federal Court in Victoria is appointed as the new Aboriginal Land Commissioner to replace Justice Olney.

AUGUST ➢ Topsy Nelson Napurrula, the CLC delegate for Ngappamilarnu and CLC Director Kumantjayi Ross travel to Geneva to participate in the annual meeting of the United Nations Working Group on Indigenous Populations.

➢ The CLC meets near Daguragu and delegates join the Gurindji in a celebration to mark the twenty-fifth anniversary of the Gurindji walkoff. Five hundred people attend including writer Frank Hardy and former prime minister Gough Whitlam.

SEPTEMBER ➢ The Aboriginal Land Commissioner recommends that the vast majority of the North-West Simpson Desert land claim be returned to traditional landowners.

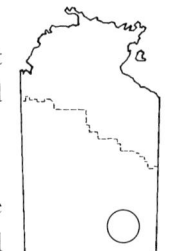

➢ CLC Director Kumanjayi Ross is appointed as a part-time ATSIC Commissioner by the Minister for Aboriginal Affairs.

OCTOBER ➢ Mr Long Pwerle is re-elected as Chairman at the CLC meeting at Arraculara. Barry Abbott, an Arrernte man representing Wallace Rockhole, is elected as Deputy Chairman.

➢ The AAPA informs the Power and Water Authority (PAWA) that it cannot issue an authority certificate for the construction of the re-designed dam at Junction Waterhole. PAWA applies to the Minister for Lands and Housing Mr Max Ortmann for a review of the AAPA decision.

➢ The CLC and Warlpiri traditional landowners sign an exploration agreement with the Tanami Joint Venturers for fourteen square kilometres of land in the Tanami Desert.

GURINDJI 25 YEARS

On 25 August 1991, over 500 people gathered at Gordy Creek to celebrate the twenty-fifth anniversary of the Gurindji walkoff and the victories it sparked.

Victor Vincent, whose father led the walkoff, told the crowd about the strength that led the Gurindji to freedom in their own land.

'My father couldn't read and write but he was really clever and he talked to the manager really strong', said Mr Vincent. 'He knew the tribal law and fought for the tribal law.

'He told the station manager, 'I think we need to work more good way and with more wages'. But the station just offered him two dollars a week.

'You know two dollars? You can't buy clothes you can't buy anything. So he said 'No — I'm gone. I'm gonna take all the people and go. I'm finished with Wave Hill''.

Political activist and author Frank Hardy, who helped to publicise the walkoff and to organise support for the Gurindji's struggle, told the celebration that the walkoff 'was the most important thing I ever got involved in.'

'Sometimes I was quite afraid that people would come with guns to get them out, but they stayed there and finally they got the land.

'Maybe they've still got problems and worries, but the Gurindji never yet struck a worry they couldn't beat or a problem they couldn't get round.'

Many of those who led the walkoff have now passed away but Mick Rangiari and the other community members who remember those days joined former Prime Minister Gough Whitlam, Aboriginal Affairs Minister Robert Tickner and Central Land Council delegates at the Daguragu celebration. Singer Paul Kelly performed *From little things big things grow,* the song he and Kev Carmody wrote about the walkoff.

Led by children from Daguragu, the Gurindji and their guests retraced part of their original walk in a re-enactment that they have observed since 1984.

As the sun set Gurindji men and women, and women from Lajamanu and Papunya danced and sang to celebrate the land that has been won back and the struggle that began it.

1991

➤ Titles for two areas of land totalling 3,682 square kilometres are handed back to traditional landowners at Piccaninny Bore, 600 kilometres north-west of Alice Springs. The areas are part of the land claimed by Gurindji, Nyininyi and Warlpiri traditional owners in the Western Desert land claim. The claim was lodged in May 1980.

➤ North Flinders Mine announces the discovery of a high-grade gold deposit on Aboriginal land in the Tanami Desert. The Callie deposit is four times richer than the average grade for Australian open-cut mines and contains an estimated 710,000 ounces of gold. Exploration was conducted under an agreement reached between NFM and the CLC on 28 September 1990.

Sadly, within some sections of the mining industry, there appears to be little understanding of the interests of Aboriginal people and too few

KINGS CANYON LODGE

The $17-million Kings Canyon Frontier Lodge was the end result of years of negotiation and development by the CLC and traditional landowners. The project was financed by the Aboriginal and Torres Strait Islander Commercial Development Corporation (ATSICDC) and Centrecorp – the investment company established by CLC, Congress and Tangentyere Council – in partnership with Frontier Holidays.

ATSICDC Chairman Gatjil Djerrkura described the project, which was the corporation's first major investment, as a landmark: 'It's the beginning of Aboriginal involvement in the commercial–industrial world – becoming an equal contributor in the Australian economy.'

Australian Frontier's Trevor Burslem explained that his company's partnership with Aboriginal people makes good business sense.

'It's quite logical for us because firstly, the traditional owners have special access to particular areas and secondly, there's a growing demand, particularly from overseas visitors who want to learn more about Aboriginal culture and life.'

The opening in October 1991 was attended by traditional landowners from local communities at Lilla, Ukaka, Wanmara and Ulpanyali. The local communities are using the resort not only as a direct source of employment but also as a focus for their own small business ventures, including arts and crafts, guided tours and trail rides.

1991

people willing to make an effort to find out what Aboriginal interests in the land really are.

The problem with many mining companies is that they assume they know what Aboriginal people want, without discussing it with the people concerned.

North Flinders Mines' people have done that from day one – sitting around the campfires discussing the interests of the people with the people and their representatives, the Central Land Council.

Discussing their concerns about our activity, and occasionally dispelling some misconceptions which may have arisen through the ventures – or sometimes misadventures – of other mining companies.
Geoff Stewart, Chief Executive North Flinders Mines.

➤ The Kings Canyon Frontier Lodge is officially opened by senior traditional landowner Peter Bulla, Aboriginal Affairs Minister Robert Tickner and Northern Territory Minister for Industries and Development Steve Hatton. The $17-million project was jointly funded by the Aboriginal and Torres Strait Islander Commercial Development Corporation, Centrecorp and Frontier Holidays.

➤ Title to the Finke land claim (5,437 square kilometres of land in the south-western Simpson Desert near the Northern Territory–South Australian border) is handed back to the Southern Arrernte traditional landowners.

DECEMBER

It's important to get the title for that country. That's my land and I got to go back that way. We're ready to go back and stop there.'
Brownie Doolan.

➤ The CLC meets with other Aboriginal, community, environment, industry and government representatives to discuss the future of the Aboriginal pastoral industry. The workshop focuses on developing a strategy to develop successful Aboriginal-owned cattle projects in the Northern Territory.

➤ The Barunga Statement is hung in Parliament House, Canberra, in fulfilment of the promise made by Prime Minister Bob Hawke in 1988. The hanging is Mr Hawke's last official act as Prime Minister and is attended by the Central and Northern Land Council executives.

FOR PRIME MINSTERS TO SEE, UNDERSTAND AND HONOUR

The hanging of the Barunga Statement on 20 December 1991 was Bob Hawke's last official duty as Prime Minister of Australia. The ceremony, which was attended by the Central and Northern Land Council executives, fulfilled a promise made by Mr Hawke to hang the Statement in the Australian Parliament 'for Prime Ministers of this country to not only see, but to understand and honour'.

Mr Hawke said the presence of the Barunga Statement in Parliament House will place an obligation on all future governments.

> It demands of them that they continue efforts to find solutions to the problems, the abundant problems that still face Aboriginal people in this country. While I take enormous pride in what we have achieved no-one talking of a problem of these dimensions could believe that you have gone anywhere near far enough.
>
> And in a sense I look to you my Aboriginal friends to say yes you have done well but also please to understand the sense of disappointment in a way that I have, that more could not have been done; because there is no group of people in our country who deserve more of the country than our Aboriginal people.

Mr Hawke nominated the Royal Commission into Aboriginal Deaths in Custody and the Council of Aboriginal Reconciliation as the two major achievements of his Government for Aboriginal people.

He urged all state and territory governments to join the Commonwealth in acting on the 339 recommendations of the Royal Commission.

'There is no greater moral obligation on the governments of this country than to pick up those recommendations and act on them,' said Mr Hawke.

He said that Australia could not go proudly into the next century unless there was reconciliation.

> Personally, I would like to see that embodied in a document. I think it is infinitely more preferable that we have the courage to do that, but it is also true that the document itself in one sense is not the important thing. The important thing is what is in our minds and in our hearts.

1992

JANUARY

➤ The Aboriginal Areas Protection Authority informs Lands and Housing Minister Max Ortmann that, after reviewing its decision, it stands by its refusal to issue a certificate for work on the Junction Waterhole dam.

FEBRUARY

➤ The Aboriginal Pastoral Working Party meets for the first time. The Working Party is an initiative from Aboriginal Pastoralists Conference held in Katherine in December 1991 and includes representatives from the Central and Northern Land Councils, ATSIC, the Commonwealth and Northern Territory Governments, the Northern Territory Cattlemen's Association and Greening Australia.

MARCH

➤ The Land Commissioner recommends that the entire Tanami Downs land claim area be returned to traditional landowners.

➤ The Minister for Lands and Housing Max Ortmann announces that he will override the decision of the AAPA and issue a certificate authorising work to proceed on the prposed Junction Waterhole dam. He admits in his statement to the Northern Territory Legislative Assembly that the dam will destroy sacred sites and that custodians oppose the project.

On 13 March Mr Ortmann and the Minister for Aboriginal Affairs Robert Tickner meet with custodians near Junction Waterhole. When the discussion becomes heated Mr Ortmann insults the custodians and walks out of the meeting.

➤ On 20 March Mr Tickner issues an emergency declaration to stop work on the dam for thirty days, using his powers under the *Aboriginal and Torres Strait Islander Heritage Protection Act*.

The dam site is a very sacred thing and we cannot say much about it. Our Dreamtime is what keeps us. It is something that is really alive. We don't need the dam. The old people are saying it. Everybody is saying it. The whole town knows, even the children. It is going to cover a whole lot of areas. Children will not be able to see those things, or hear the stories that go with them. They are very strong and need to be kept sacred.
Agnes Palmer, a custodian for Junction Waterhole

➤ The CLC learns that Mr Carl Strehlow is trying to sell a substantial number of sacred objects collected by his late father, Professor Ted Strehlow. Most of the objects were taken from the CLC region of Central Australia and under Aboriginal Law are owned by the traditional landowners. The CLC approaches the South Australian Government and Mr Strehlow.

1992

➤ The CLC opens a western regional office based in Papunya.

➤ The CLC and the Northern Territory Police Force (Southern Division) jointly announce new police procedures to prevent the release of names and photos of deceased Aboriginal people to the media. Aboriginal people avoid using the names or images of deceased people as a mark of respect and bereavement, and the publication of names and photos in media reports about tragedies has often caused great offence and distress to family and community members. The CLC welcomes the police decision to withhold these details as 'a sign of the police force's growing sensitivity to Aboriginal cultural values.'

APRIL ➤ The Minister for Aboriginal and Torres Strait Islander Affairs Robert Tickner appoints the Hal Wootten QC to prepare a report on whether the proposed Junction Waterhole dam should be stopped under s.10 of the *Aboriginal and Torres Strait Islander Heritage Protection Act*. Mr Wootten is a former Royal Commissioner into Aboriginal Deaths in Custody. The Minister extends the temporary stop on work to sixty days to provide time for Mr Wootten's inquiry, which considers submissions from all parties.

➤ The CLC meets with government agencies and industry groups to examine the long-term prospects for industries based on camel products. A number of communities in the CLC region are interested in developing camel enterprises but have found only limited market opportunities. The CLC joined a steering committee to examine means to develop this industry.

➤ The Power and Water Authority (PAWA) disconnects electricity at Kaltukatjara (Docker River) and Yuendumu. Although their power costs are being paid by Commonwealth grants, the Northern Territory Government is determined to force remote Aboriginal users to pay for their household power. In both Kaltukatjara and Yuendumu the whole community is disconnected – individual householders have never been approached to sign on as PAWA customers. It is almost three weeks before the power is reconnected so that individual households can make their own decisions.

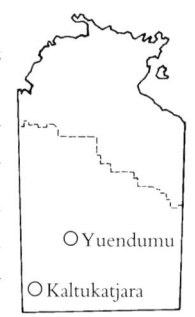

➤ The South Australian Minister for Environment and Planning orders Carl Strehlow to surrender the sacred objects he has offered for sale. The objects are photographed and catalogued by the South Australian Department of Environment and Planning and the Northern Territory Government's Strehlow Research Centre. The CLC employs a consultant anthropologist to identify and consult the Aboriginal owners of the objects.

1992

➤ On 22 April 1992 the Chairman of the Central Land Council, Mr Long Pwerle, passed away at his home in Alekarenge. He had been Chairman of the CLC since 1988. Mr Long Pwerle was forty-six years old.

MAY

➤ Titles for two Aboriginal-owned pastoral properties – McLaren Creek and Ti-Tree – are handed back. Ti-Tree Station, 200 kilometres north of Alice Springs, was purchased in 1976 by the Aboriginal Land Fund. McLaren Creek, 100 kilometres south of Tennant Creek, was purchased in April 1985 with money earned through mining on Aboriginal land.

➤ The Minister for Aboriginal and Torres Strait Islander Affairs Robert Tickner issues a declaration to protect the complex of sacred sites near Junction Waterhole for twenty years and prevent the construction of the proposed dam under s.10 of the *Aboriginal and Torres Strait Islander Heritage Protection Act*. The Minister's action follows the recommendations of the Hal Wootten who was appointed to inquire into the issue.

The dreamings that form these sites connect Aboriginal groups throughout the region. Luritja, Ngaanyatjarra, Pitjantjatjara, Warlpiri, Warumungu and Yankunytjatjarta people have all actively supported the Arrernte custodians throughout their long fight to defend these sacred sites.
Today's decision is a turning point. Too often in the past the development of Alice Springs has been at the expense of the Aboriginal people. Sacred sites have been destroyed and desecrated and the protests of Aboriginal people have been rubbished and ignored. Now at last we have seen some justice.
Kumantjayi Ross, CLC Director

➤ Papunya community meets with Power and Water Authority (PAWA) representatives to discuss the Northern Territory Government's new power billing system. Community members are angry that they are being asked to pay while the non-Aboriginal employees who live in Papunya get their power free of charge. The community meeting tells PAWA they would rather go without electricity than pay, and Papunya householders refuse to sign connection forms.

The Power and Water Authority meet with Papunya residents to discuss the new power billing system.

MR LONG PWERLE

Mr Long Pwerle was first elected Chairman of the CLC in November 1988, and re-elected for another three-year term in October 1992. From 1973 to 1976 Mr Long had been a member of the National Aboriginal Consultative Committee and he was a member of the Aboriginal Benefit Trust Account from 1980. Mr Long Pwerle died in April 1992.

'This great leader has been an example of a younger Central Australian leadership and shown us a different side,' said NLC Chairman Galarrwuy Yunupingu. 'We're going to miss him because through him the Central and Northern Land Councils have created a firmer relationship.'

CLC Director Kumantjayi Ross described Mr Long Pwerle as a man of magnetic charm.

'Like all great leaders he brought people together,' said Mr Ross. 'People from different communities and languages, Aboriginal and non-Aboriginal. So many times I saw him turn around a meeting and smooth out differences so that people put the differences aside and worked together.

'He led the CLC successfully through some of its most important struggles and under his leadership the Land Council remained unified and strong.'

Mr Long Pwerle was a skilled communicator and advocate for Aboriginal people. He spoke nine Aboriginal languages – Alyawarr, Anmatyerre, Eastern Arrernte, Western Arrernte, Kaytetye, Luritja, Pitjantjatjara, Warlpiri and Warumungu – as well as English. He maintained a close association with people on the land and continued to live and work at Alekarenge. His deep understanding of the issues in the bush enabled him to get the message across to governments and other non-Aboriginal groups, and bridge the gap between Aboriginal and non-Aboriginal politics.

Mr Long Pwerle pushed the Commonwealth Government to honour its promise to hang the Barunga Statement and led the CLC meeting at Intjartnama which gave its timely backing to the process of reconciliation in April 1991.

'Mr Long gave me a handful of dirt to take back to Parliament House from that Intjartnama meeting,' said Aboriginal Affairs Minister Robert Tickner.

'I took that dirt with me into the Cabinet room that night to help me get further endorsement for the reconciliation process to go forward into the Parliament.

'I've met many people across the country but there are few who've had such strong personal impact on me and my staff as Mr Long. He was a person who always showed great leadership and sensitivity and who worked from a great commitment for his people. His strength and conviction will remain with us always.'

1992

➢ The Central Land Council elects Mr Kunmanara Breaden as Chairman at the Council's meeting at Atnwengerrp. Mr Breaden is a Luritja man who lives at Wanmara, near Kings Canyon. He was a founding member of the CLC and served as Deputy Chairman between 1980 and 1986, and Acting Chairman in 1986.

A lot of people in Central Australia are still waiting for their land and for excisions on pastoral land. As Chairman I'm going to be strong and push for all those Aboriginal people who have nothing.'
Kunmanara Breaden, CLC Chairman

➢ The South Australian Department of Environment and Planning seizes sacred objects and other material from the office and residence of Mrs Kathleen Strehlow, the widow of Professor Ted Strehlow.

JUNE

➢ On 3 June 1992 the High Court overturns the doctrine of terra nullius and recognises the existence of native title in the case of *Eddie Mabo and Others v the State of Queensland*. The decision brings Australian common law into line with international precedents and historical fact, by recognising the Aboriginal and Torres Strait Islanders had, and in some cases still have, property rights in their traditional lands.

➢ The Northern Territory Aboriginal Pastoral Industry Working Group initiates a major research project to support Aboriginal cattle enterprises and develop management plans for Aboriginal-owned pastoral properties.

➢ The Northern Territory Ombudsman finds that the Power and Water Authority (PAWA) misled Hermannsburg residents when they signed on as customers. At a community meeting the residents were told that their first bill would only be a 'sample' bill and not for payment. Later PAWA told the community that residents would not only have to pay the first bill but would have to pay for power used since April – six weeks before they signed on. PAWA eventually agrees to start charging from 1 July.

➢ More than sixty women from the CLC region join Aboriginal women from Western Australia, South Australia and other parts of the Northern Territory in a five-day meeting of celebration and ceremony at Yukawala Bore, south of Halls Creek.

JULY

➢ Thirteen communities from the CLC region meet together at Papunya to form the One United Voice Association. The Association, sparked by the PAWA billing dispute, will promote greater autonomy for communities. Representatives from One United Voice join other Aboriginal com-

THE POWER DISPUTE

The power dispute crystallised many of the differences between the Northern Territory Government and remote Aboriginal communities in Central Australia. Even though the Government first signalled its intention to introduce individual household billing in 1987, it didn't consult remote Aboriginal householders about the change and some knew nothing of the billing system until after their power was disconnected.

Many community members had serious concerns about the new system: how would they find the extra money on their limited incomes, how would the user-pays system deal with the highly mobile populations, why should Aboriginal householders pay if non-Aboriginal community workers don't and why was the change being introduced if the Commonwealth was willing to pay the bill anyhow?

None of these issues were addressed before the changes were introduced. Alison Anderson, the Administration Officer at Papunya Community Council and a traditional landowner, explained the real power issues in an open letter at the height of the dispute.

> *We the Community at Papunya feel that there is more at issue than simply the power supply to people's houses. To us the problem is much more and involves the issue of power being given to the people themselves.*
>
> *The history of Papunya, and many other settlements like ours, is a history of decisions being made by others and not the people directly affected by these decisions.*
>
> *The central area of Papunya settlement was originally built as an administration and accommodation area for non-Aboriginal people who came to work here. These people wanted a style of life which they were used to, therefore they wanted power generation. In the early years we lived without power and were not even allowed into this area after work time.*
>
> *Many people here still live without power.*
>
> *Power lines run everywhere at Papunya because it was someone else's plan how Papunya settlement would grow and how it should look. Aboriginal people had other ideas but we were never asked.*
>
> *Right from the start Europeans have never had to pay for their power and this is still the same today. Now as Aboriginal people begin to move into this area and have their houses connected to power they are told they must pay. We wonder why the difference.*
>
> *We are told we should be treated equally like other people. This we would be happy with but we do not think we are being treated equally at all.*
>
> *We do not have work opportunities equal to Europeans. Our laws and customs are not treated equally as Europeans. Those of us who do have jobs do not have equal wages and conditions like the Europeans who work here. Our children are not obtaining equal levels of education as European children and we are not given equal opportunity to make decisions over our own lives as the rest of the Australian population.*
>
> *This is the real power issue at Papunya.*

1992

munity leaders to meet with the Commonwealth Grants Commission in late July to push for Commonwealth grants to be paid directly to communities rather than channelled through the Northern Territory Government.

➤ A consultant anthropologist reports that most Aboriginal custodians want sacred objects collected by Professor Ted Strehlow returned. The report identifies the custodians and rightful owners for over 150 sacred objects offered for sale by Professor Strehlow's son, Carl. In the overwhelming majority of cases the custodians asked for the objects to be returned directly to their control.

These objects are part of a living Aboriginal culture and law. Now that the custodians have been located and properly consulted there can be no question that the objects must be dealt with in accordance with their wishes.
Kumantjayi Ross, CLC Director

➤ The CLC and the Northern Territory Government negotiate an agreement to settle the Kanturrpa–Kanttaji land claim without the need for a hearing before the Aboriginal Land Commissioner. The historic agreement provides for 150 square kilometres to be granted as Aboriginal land under the Land Rights Act, with public access to Cabbage Gum Bore and a guaranteed water supply for Tennant Creek.

➤ CLC Chairman Kunmanara Breaden leads a delegation including Deputy Director Tracker Tilmouth and artist Frank Nelson Jakamarra to attend the tenth session of the United Nations Working Group on Indigenous Populations tenth session in Geneva. They present a replica of the Barunga statement and a painting by Mr Nelson to the WGIP Chairperson, Madame Erica Daes.

AUGUST

➤ Mistake Creek Cattle Station sells 1,300 Brahman-cross steers to Indonesia in an export contract worth $300,000.

1992

➢ The Northern Territory Government takes legal action to assert ownership of the sacred objects and other material collected by Professor Ted Strehlow which was surrendered and seized by the South Australian Government. The Northern Territory Government claims that the objects belong in its Strehlow Research Centre. The CLC meeting at Mistake Creek, west of Katherine condemns the Northern Territory Government's action and calls for the return of objects to Aboriginal control.

SEPTEMBER ➢ Some members of the 'Variety Club Bash', a charity car rally, drive around Uluru in breach of the park rules. Their action, which causes great offence to traditional landowners, is encouraged by three Northern Territory Government ministers travelling with the bash as a way of highlighting their dissatisfaction with Aboriginal control of the Park.

OCTOBER ➢ Aboriginal pastoralists from the CLC region meet at Hamilton Downs to discuss the development of management plans, an industry strategy and the work of the Northern Territory Aboriginal Pastoral Industry Working Group.

➢ The CLC opens an eastern regional office at Atnwengerrp.

➢ The CLC meeting at Atula elects Rex Granites Japanangka to replace Barry Abbott as Deputy Chairman.

➢ Governor-General Bill Hayden hands back title for 4,000 square kilometres of land to traditional owners for the Wakaya–Alyawarr land claim. The handback ceremony at Purukwarurr, south-east of Tennant Creek, is the second attended by a governor-general. The first was the Uluru–Kata Tjuta handback in 1985.

NOVEMBER ➢ Chief Minister Marshall Perron announces that his government will provide $600,000 in funding to any Aboriginal group willing to establish breakaway land councils to breakdown the power of the CLC and NLC.

What Mr Perron wants everyone to forget is that the CLC and NLC are representative organisations with statutory responsibilities to protect Aboriginal people's rights and represent the wishes of Aboriginal land owners.
What seems to upset Mr Perron about the land councils is that we're good at our job.
Kumantjayi Ross, CLC Director

MCLAREN CREEK

In January 1977 the Alyawarr walked off Kurundi Station. More than ten years after the equal pay case and the Gurindji walkoff, Aboriginal pastoral workers were still getting little more than rations, and workers who tried to insist on correct pay and conditions were often simply 'taken to the bitumen', and told to walk into town. Poor accommodation, health and education services added to the discontent at Kurundi, but land was a central issue and the Kurundi mob took their concerns to the CLC's first meeting under the new Land Rights Act in February 1977.

Since the early 1970s the Warumungu had been trying to purchase Kurundi and McLaren Creek Station. After the walkoff the largest of the family groups involved decided to sit down on a water reserve at Ngurrutiji, about sixty kilometres north of Kurundi. Murphy Japanangka summed up the aims of the 'Ngurrutiji mob' back in 1977:

> *All my life, I've worked for other people and now I want this piece of land to live on and break horses for ourselves. I'm not working for Kurundi again without a contract. We should be paid holiday money, but we got nothing. We need to look around and find a really good place to make a permanent camp where we can build proper houses. Ngurrutiji is good for now, but I don't know whether we will always camp here. We will always look after it. Until we have our horses and things off Kurundi and at Ngurrutiji, we really can't think about what to do next.**

Ngurrutiji was claimed as part of the Warumungu land claim and became caught up in the endless Northern Territory Government legal challenges and obstruction that delayed its handback for fifteen years. In the meantime the Ngurrutiji mob were central to the development of McLaren Creek.

The lease to McLaren Creek Station was purchased by Mungkarta Pastoral Company on behalf of the traditional landowners in 1985, using money earned from mining on Aboriginal land. The station was overrun with feral horses and severely degraded but the traditional landowners drew on their highly developed pastoral skills to muster the horses and repair the station infrastructure with a minimum of equipment.

The Ngurrutiji mob turned their adversity to advantage and used the restoration of McLaren to train young workers in the old stock skills while teaching them the stories of their country.

'We like this job,' said Murphy Japanangka. 'We like to do bore and cattle work and brumby horse. I know how to work the cattle station since I was a kid. All these young fellas I've been teaching them and now they are working and working. Sometimes I've got to growl, but these young fellas out there are doing a good job for me and when you're working like that you can grow the station up.'

The title to McLaren Creek Station was eventually handed back in May 1992.

'I'm happy tonight,' said Japanangka after the handover. 'I've been doing the job here and waiting for a long time – for fifteen years now. Now we've got the title to McLaren Creek.'

---

* Dianne Bell, 'For Our Families: the Kurundi walk off and the Nurrantiji venture', *Aboriginal History*, 2(1), 1978.

1992

➤ Traditional landowners buy Loves Creek pastoral lease with the assistance of the CLC and a land claim is lodged on behalf of traditional landowners.

➤ The Central Australian Aboriginal Investment Corporation (CAIC) enters a joint venture with Peter Kittle Toyota and Peter Kittle Mitsubishi. The investment company is an independent corporation backed by the CLC and other Aboriginal organisations to promote long-term investments for the Aboriginal community.

➤ Chief Minister Marshall Perron states in a speech to the Legislative Assembly that his government is willing to settle all outstanding land claims. The CLC says that it is willing to discuss genuine offers but will wait to see the detail of Mr Perron's proposal. In a cabinet reshuffle Mr Perron appoints Steve Hatton as Minister for Aboriginal Development.

➤ Arrernte, Anmatyerre, Pitjantjatjara, Ngaanyatjarra and Yankunytjatjara women from Central Australia meet to celebrate their victory in stopping the proposed dam at Junction Waterhole six months earlier.

➤ Three years after the Memorandum of Agreement on living areas the Northern Territory Government approves the first new excision in the CLC region. The small living area on Huckitta Station was approved after agreement was negotiated between the traditional landowners and the pastoralist.

DECEMBER ➤ Prime Minister Paul Keating speaks at Redfern Park, Sydney, to mark the start of the Year of Indigenous People.

By doing away with the bizarre conceit that this continent had no owners prior to the settlement of Europeans, Mabo establishes a fundamental truth and lays the basis for justice.
It will be much easier to work from that basis than has ever been the case in the past.
For that reason alone we should ignore the isolated outbreaks of hysteria and hostility of the past few months.

1992

Mabo is an historic decision – we can make it an historic turning point, the basis of a new relationship between indigenous and non-Aboriginal Australians.

The message should be that there is nothing to fear or to lose in the recognition of historical truth, or the extension of social justice, or the deepening of Australian social democracy to include indigenous Australians.

There is everything to gain.
Prime Minister Paul Keating, 10 December 1992

➤ The title for Kunoth Bore and Mount Solitaire stock reserves are handed back to traditional landowners. These are the last of twenty-six stock reserves and stock route sections in the CLC region handed back under the 1989 Memorandum of Agreement between Prime Minister Bob Hawke and Chief Minister Marshall Perron. The handbacks represent the fulfilment of the Commonwealth's side of that agreement, but despite three years of applications not a single new community living area has been created for Aboriginal people by the Northern Territory Government. Aboriginal Affairs Minister Robert Tickner frequently criticises the Northern Territory Government's failure but the Commonwealth takes no stronger action despite its constitutional power to do so.

➤ Title to 3,090 square kilometres of the Warumungu land claim area is handed back at Kurraya outstation, east of Tennant Creek. This is the second part of the Warumungu lands to be returned but does not include the areas recommended for grant near Tennant Creek town boundaries.

I was happy to get the land, but sad that the relatives that started the fight for the title passed away without seeing it come back to their kids and their grandchildren.
Our main aim now in town is to teach the Europeans about our black history and what's happened there so they can fully understand why the land has been handed back, so we can work in with the community for our kids and for everyone. We want to keep a strong tie with the land and the culture.
Ross Williams, Warumungu traditional landowner

1993

FEBRUARY ➢ Four Aboriginal women backed by the Northern Territory Government apply to the Federal Court to prevent the Aboriginal Affairs Minister Tickner from handing back title to areas recommended for grant in the Lake Amadeus land claim. Their action is the first 'Mabo-style' assertion of native title but ironically it attempts to prevent title being given to traditional landowners.

MARCH ➢ Title to 290 square kilometres of land near Tennant Creek township is handed back to the Warumungu traditional landowners by Aboriginal Affairs Minister Robert Tickner. The traditional landowners have given up a large area of land adjoining the town boundary to provide for possible town expansion. In return the traditional landowners are promised title to two areas containing important sacred sites — Kunjarra (Devils Pebbles) and Junkurakurr — and reach a joint management agreement with Tennant Creek Town Council for the Mary Ann Dam Reserve.

It's a great occasion. So many people fought so long for the land. A lot of people have passed away, but they're still with us and they're still with the land.
Now its up to us to go back and establish ourselves on those lands and develop something so that we don't have to rely on government funding, but rely on building something for ourselves.
Ross Williams, Warumungu traditional owner

➢ Vandals paint racist slogans on the Warumungu mural outside the CLC's Tennant Creek office. CLC Assistant Director Tracker Tilmouth condemns the attack as a bitter affront to Aboriginal and non-Aboriginal people and out of step with the broader community in Tennant Creek.

1993

➤Ian Conway, the tourist operator at Kings Creek Station, makes an offer to settle the Lake Amadeus land claim. Mr Conway's business was established on land illegally leased to him by the Northern Territory Government, and his subsequent investment has become an obstacle to the handback of the land recommended for grant. Although the CLC and traditional landowners respond positively to the offer, no settlement can be reached because of the pending Federal Court case.

➤Prime Minister Keating and the Labor Government are re-elected in a victory that runs against the predictions of opinion polls and pundits. Robert Tickner remains Minister for Aboriginal and Torres Strait Islander Affairs but his ministry is transferred to report directly to the Prime Minister and Special Minister of State Frank Walker is given responsibility for dealing with the implications of the Mabo decision.

➤The Northern Territory Government and the CLC agree to a tourist permit system for the Mereenie/Watarrka road. The upgrading of the road will benefit the tourist industry and in particular Aboriginal tourist enterprises at Wallace Rockhole, Hermannsburg, Ipolera, Glen Helen and Watarrka (Kings Canyon). The traditional landowners and CLC have been involved in negotiations over the road for some time but the Northern Territory Government had been reluctant to allow traditional landowners to maintain their control over access to their land.

APRIL

➤The CLC joins other major Aboriginal organisations in sending a delegation to meet with Prime Minister Keating and other ministers to discuss the implications of the High Court's Mabo decision. The delegation presents a painting by former CLC Chairman Wenten Rubuntja and puts a peace plan to the Prime Minister.

I'm more than convinced than ever that we've got to make peace with the Aborigines to get the place right.
Paul Keating addressing his staff on the eve of the 1993 Federal Election

Photo: Peter West AUSPIC

1993

JULY ➤ The title for 190 square kilometres recommended for grant in the Warumungu land claim is handed over at Cabbage Gum Bore. The handback is the fourth part of Warumungu to be returned. At the same ceremony the title to the 150-square-kilometre Kanturrpa–Kanttaji land claim area is returned. The area was scheduled as Aboriginal land under an agreement reached between the Northern Territory Government and the CLC without completing the claim process.

➤ At a press conference in Sydney, Chief Minister Perron tells the Foreign Correspondents Association that Aboriginal culture is 'centuries behind' European culture because Aboriginal people aren't driven by 'the desire for material possessions'.

➤ The CLC signs an exploration agreement with the Sons of Gwalia Ltd at Mt Theo outstation, 400 kilometres north-west of Alice Springs. The agreement covers 4,444 square kilometres of land.

This new company, Sons of Gwalia, took the right approach. They met with traditional owners and explained what they wanted to do. They didn't put pressure on people and they listened to what Aboriginal people were saying to them.
We're happy they'll be here and we'll be working closely with them. We're hoping some of our young people will be trained and will be employed in the future.
Rex Granites Japanangka

➤ The CLC begins a major land assessment program covering large areas of Aboriginal land in central and northern Australia. The project, which is funded by ATSIC and the National Landcare Program, will involve Anangu Pitjantjatjara, the Kimberley Land Council and the NLC and use computer-based land information systems to plan sustainable development on Aboriginal land.

AUGUST ➤ CLC representatives join hundreds of Aboriginal people from throughout Australia at a national meeting at Eva Valley, near Katherine, to discuss the High Court's Mabo decision.

1993

➤The CLC signs an exploration agreement with Kunapula Pty Ltd — a company which is one hundred per cent owned by traditional landowners from Kaltukatjara (Docker River). The agreement, which was signed at Tjunti outstation, covers a 161-square-kilometre area south of Kaltukatjara.

➤The CLC and Warlpiri traditional landowners sign an exploration agreement with North Flinders Mines at Lajamanu. The agreement covers more than 3,000 square kilometres in the Tanami Desert — one of Australia's richest gold-bearing regions.

SEPTEMBER

➤Two sacred sites are destroyed during boundary work for a new national park. The Northern Territory Government is purchasing the land for the Davenport–Murchison Ranges National Park from Kurundi Station but has not consulted the traditional landowners despite their important sacred site and native title interests in the area.

➤The Northern Territory Chief Minister, Marshall Perron, writes to Prime Minister Paul Keating, offering a 'once and for all resolution' of Aboriginal land issues in the Northern Territory. He calls for an end to Aboriginal control over exploration and mining on Aboriginal land in exchange for the Northern Territory Government's agreement to allow some existing land claims to be converted to Aboriginal land without going through the land claim process.

Now Mr Perron has the hide to suggest that the NT Government will stop obstructing land claims on condition that vital rights such as inalienable title and the right to consent to development are ripped out of the Land Rights Act.
If the NT Government was serious about resolving land needs for Aboriginal people they would take immediate action to ensure that Aboriginal people living in desperate need on pastoral leases could obtain proper title to living areas on their land.
CLC Director Kumantjayi Ross

➤The Commonwealth Government releases a draft outline of its proposed legislation regarding the High Court's Mabo decision. The proposal validates and protects non-Aboriginal land interests at the expense of Aboriginal land rights. It overrides the Racial Discrimination Act and will extinguish native title to validate non-Aboriginal titles even if the Government's acted in breach of its fiduciary responsibility in granting these titles. Native title would also be extinguished on pastoral leases and national parks even though there may be no conflict between the rights of native title and the rights of the other titleholders.

1993

Unlike the Land Rights Act the proposal does not give native title holders the power to control access by miners and other developers onto their land – it only provides the right to negotiate.

➤ The CLC and other Aboriginal organisations hold a two-day meeting of Central Australian Aboriginal people to discuss the Commonwealth Government's draft legislation. The meeting rejects key parts of the draft including the proposal to override the Racial Discrimination Act, to extinguish native title on pastoral leases and national parks and the lack of Aboriginal control over access and development. CLC representatives then travel to Canberra to join a national Aboriginal meeting on Mabo. Central Australian artist Michael Nelson Jagamarra threatens to remove the mosaic from the forecourt of Parliament House which is based on his painting.

The Government does not respect my painting or my people. I want to take my painting back to my people. If the government does not listen to Aboriginal people then we will all take the painting home.

➤ The Federal Court rejects a Northern Territory Government backed legal action to use native title rights to prevent the handback of land recommended for grant in the Lake Amadeus land claim.

OCTOBER ➤ Following representations from the CLC and other land councils Prime Minister Paul Keating announces that the Government will not override the Racial Discrimination Act in its Native Title legislation. The decision is a major turning point in the negotiations.

➤ The President of the Australian Council of Trade Unions Martin Ferguson travels to Central Australia to visit mining projects on Aboriginal land and talk with traditional landowners and miners.

There are practical people out there in both the mining industry and amongst the traditional landowners who want jobs and who want mining to occur.
I walk away with the view that frankly those traditional landowners are not opposed to mining at all. All they are seeking is that in the process of developing a mine site that there be an opportunity for proper discussions, and, I suppose, a requirement that they be treated with some dignity so that the issues of concern and importance to them are taken into consideration in the development of the mining industry in this country.

1993

DECEMBER

➢Warlpiri traditional landowners sign a mineral exploration agreement for an area of 2,576 square kilometres near Willowra, 300 kilometres northwest of Alice Springs. A total of 42,000 square kilometres in the CLC region is now being explored and mined under the Land Rights Act.

Photo: Centralian Advocate

Aboriginal people with the right of consent over development on their land are using that right judiciously and effectively to achieve controlled development.
This right is vital for Aboriginal people. It allows them to manage the pace of development, to protect sacred sites and the environment and it enables them to successfully negotiate agreements which give them a fair deal and employment opportunities in the industry.
The process of laid out for negotiating exploration agreements under the Land Rights Act works for mining companies too. they know exactly where they stand at every stage – there is no uncertainty, no disputation.
Acting CLC Director Tracker Tilmouth

➢ATSIC purchases Tempe Downs Station on behalf of the Luritja traditional landowners. The Luritja established one of Central Australia's first land rights organisations – the Luritja Land Association – in 1974 and have worked with the CLC and made numerous approaches to the Department of Aboriginal Affairs and ATSIC to win back control of their country.

People are very happy. There's a lot of traditional landowners. We purchased it for the whole lot. All the traditional owners.
We might get a school at Tempe Downs later on. That's a long way though. First we need proper houses, not tin sheds but fixed houses. We need bores as well.
That's a good thing that we've got now. We've been struggling for over twenty years – before land rights started we were talking to the station owners. Now we've got the station now – we've purchased it. That's

1993

pretty good, for kids especially, for the next generation.
I think they'll have a very different life from us. They might have different ideas. They won't have the struggle we older ones have had all our lives. They'll be all right. They'll be able to go ahead and do the work they like.
CLC Chairman Kunmanara Breaden

DECEMBER 22 ➢ The Australian Parliament passes the Native Title Act after months of intense lobbying and exhaustive debate. CLC Director Kumantjayi Ross was a member of the Aboriginal group which negotiated the form of the legislation with the Government.

The legislation recognises the existence of Aboriginal people's common law right to ownership of their traditional country (native title) and establishes a system of tribunals to decide where native title exists. It gives native title the same protection against seizure without compensation that freehold title enjoys. Native title holders also have the right to negotiate over mining and exploration, but their rights are not as strong as those of traditional landowners under the Land Rights Act and the Northern Territory Government immediately calls for the Land Rights Act to be amended and weakened.

We're proper happy one with the news that we're getting the title. We want this back. It's where the old men were living before. We've been trying for the last two years, talking and talking and talking, but the Minister couldn't make up his mind and Max (the station owner) couldn't make up his mind.

Now we can live here for the rest of our lives – grow our kids up here on our proper country. If we can get houses and build up this place maybe we can get a school.

Other people can fight for their land like we did for this one, They can see what we did and fight strong like we did. We've been talking here for this place. The CLC is a very good help for people to get land rights. That's the main one, that CLC mob, to fight for land rights.

CLC Chairman Kunmanara Breaden, 1994

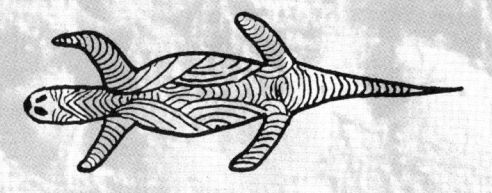

Glossary

Aboriginal and Torres Strait Islanders Commission – ATSIC
Established in 1989 to replace the Department of Aboriginal Affairs, ATSIC is based on elected regional councils and commissioners.

Aboriginal and Torres Strait Islander Heritage Protection Act
The Commonwealth Government's sacred sites protection legislation was originally passed in 1984 as an interim measure, but was extended in 1986 and continues to operate as the Commonwealth's 'backup' to inadequate state and territory legislation.

Aboriginal Areas Protection Authority – AAPA
Established under the Northern Territory Aboriginal Sacred Sites Act in 1989, it replaced the Aboriginal Sacred Sites Protection Authority. The AAPA is made up of Aboriginal and non-Aboriginal members and includes nominees from the NT land councils.

Aboriginals Benefit Trust Account – ABTA
The ABTA receives Commonwealth funds equal to 30 percent of the royalties earned from mining on Aboriginal land. An advisory committee made up of land council nominees allocates the funds to Aboriginal associations for community projects.

Aboriginal Land
Aboriginal land held under the Land Rights Act is inalienable freehold. The Act is a Commonwealth law and title is held on behalf of all the traditional landowners by an Aboriginal Land Trust.

Aboriginal Land Rights (Northern Territory) Act 1976
The Land Rights Act was passed in 1976 and came into effect on 26 January 1977. The Act establishes the basis for Aboriginal land, land claims and the land councils including the CLC.

Aboriginal Sacred Sites Protection Authority – ASSPA
Now replaced by the AAPA the Sacred Sites Authority was established by the Aboriginal Sacred Sites Act 1980.

Alienated land
Alienated land is land in which any interest (such as a lease or title) is held by an individual or corporation other than the Crown. Alienated land cannot be claimed under the Land Rights Act unless it is owned by or for Aboriginal people who agree to the claim.

Anindilyakwa Land Council
Represents the traditional landowners of Groote and Bickerton islands. Originally part of the Northern Land Council this area was established as a separate land council in 1991.

Australian Mining Industry Council – AMIC
AMIC is a mining industry lobby group that has played a leading role in campaigns against land rights throughout Australia and in particular traditional landowners' right to control access to Aboriginal land by mining and exploration companies.

Australian National Parks and Wildlife Service – ANPWS
Renamed the Australian Nature Conservation Agency in 1993 the ANPWS leases the Uluru – Kata Tjuta National Park from the traditional landowners.

Baume, Senator Peter
Minister for Aboriginal Affairs 3 November 1980 to 7 May 1982.

Breaden, Kunmanara
Chairman of the CLC from 26 May 1992 until September 1994. Mr Breaden is a Luritja man who has been fighting for land rights since before the Woodward Commission and the Land Rights Act. He has been a delegate to CLC since the land council was formed, and served as deputy

chairman from December 1980 until September 1986 and then as acting Chairman until November of that year.

Bryant, Gordon
Minister for Aboriginal Affairs 19 December 1972 to 9 October 1973.

Cavanagh, Senator James
Minister for Aboriginal Affairs 9 October 1973 to 6 June 1975.

Central Land Council – CLC
The Council first met in 1974 and became a statutory organisation under the Land Rights Act in 1977. The CLC is made up of 81 members representing 61 Aboriginal communities in central Australia. For more information read this book and *Our Land Our Life*.

Chaney, Senator Fred
Minister for Aboriginal Affairs 5 December 1978 to 3 November 1980.

Country Liberal Party – CLP
The conservative political party which has governed the Northern Territory since self-government was granted in 1978.

Department of Aboriginal Affairs – DAA
Established in 1973 to coordinate the Commonwealth Government's special programs for Aboriginal and Torres Strait Islander people, it was replaced by ATSIC in 1989.

Dodson, Patrick
Began work for the CLC in 1983 and became the CLC's first Director in 1985. Mr Dodson is a Yawuru man from Broome in the Kimberley region of Western Australia and was the first Aboriginal Catholic priest. He served as CLC Director until July 1989 when he left to work for the Kimberley Land Council and as a Commissioner for the Royal Commission into Aboriginal Deaths in Custody. In 1991 he was appointed Chairman of the Council for Aboriginal Reconciliation.

Drake-Brockman, Senator Charles
Minister for Aboriginal Affairs 12 November 1975 to 22 December 1975.

Everingham, Paul
Chief Minister of the Northern Territory from 1 July 1978 until 17 October 1984. He held the NT seat in the Federal House of Representatives from 1984 to 1987.

Finke River Mission
The Lutheran Church established the Finke River Mission at Hermannsburg in 1877. The Mission held that land as a special purpose lease until the area became Aboriginal land under the Land Rights Act.

Granites, Rex Japanangka
The current Chairman of the CLC was elected in September 1994. Mr Granites is a Warlpiri man who has served on the CLC executive and was Deputy Chairman from October 1992 until September 1994.

Hand, Gerry
Minister for Aboriginal Affairs 24 July 1987 to 4 April 1990.

Hatton, Steve
Member of the NT Legislative Assembly since 1984 holding various ministerial posts since 1985. Chief Minister of the Northern Territory from 15 May 1986 to 13 July 1988. Is now Minister for Lands and Housing, Local Government and Aboriginal Advancement.

Holding, Clyde
Minister for Aboriginal Affairs 11 March 1983 to 24 July 1987.

Howson, Peter
Minister for the Environment, Aborigines and the Arts 31 May 1971 to 5 December 1972.

Johnson, Leslie
Minister for Aboriginal Affairs 6 June 1975 to 11 November 1975.

Kearney, William
Aboriginal Land Commissioner from 1982 until 1987. Now a Judge of the Supreme Court of the Northern Territory.

Mr Long Pwerle
Mr Long was elected Chairman of the Central Land Council on 10 November 1988 and re-elected on 29 October 1991. He had worked for the CLC and on a number of bodies including the National Aboriginal Conference and the Aboriginals Benefit Trust Account. He served as CLC Chairman until his passing in April 1992.

Martin, Brian
Chaired the NT Government's inquiries into Pastoral Tenure (1980) and Sacred Sites legislation (1987). Currently Chief Justice of the NT Supreme Court.

Maurice, Michael
Aboriginal Land Commissioner from 1984 until 1987. He served concurrently with Justice William Kearney.

Northern Land Council – NLC
Represents traditional landowners in the northern part of the NT (except for those areas represented by the Tiwi and Anindilyakwa Land Councils). Like the CLC it was established during the Woodward Royal Commission and is a statutory land council under the Land Rights Act.

Olney, Howard
Aboriginal Land Commissioner from 1988 until 1991.

Perron, Marshall
Chief Minister of the Northern Territory since 14 July 1988.

Perkins, Charles
Chairman of the CLC from September 1975 until June 1976. Later head of the Aboriginal Development Corporation and the Department of Aboriginal Affairs. Currently Deputy Chairperson of ATSIC.

Ross, D. Kumantjayi
Director of the CLC from July 1989 until February 1994. Mr Ross started work with the CLC in 1979 and was appointed Assistant Director in 1988. He is a graduate in Business Management. He was appointed a part-time ATSIC Commissioner in 1991. In 1994 he resigned from the CLC to work full-time as an ATSIC Commissioner.

Rowland, Barry
Completed a review of implementation of the Land Rights Act in November 1980. Mr Rowland QC, a former Chairman of the Western Australia Law Reform Commission was appointed as a Judge of the Supreme Court of Western Australia in 1983.

Rubuntja, Wenten
CLC Chairman from 1976 to December 1980 and November 1985 to 1988. An Arrernte man born at Burt Creek, north of Alice Springs, he played a leading role in the establishment of a number of Aboriginal organisations including the CLC, the Central Australian Aboriginal Congress and Tangentyere Council. He is currently a member of the Aboriginal Reconciliation Council, the Aboriginal Areas Protection Authority and the Conservation Commission of the NT.

Scrutton, Stanley
Served as CLC Chairman from December 1980 until he resigned in September 1986.

Shaw, Geoffrey
Elected Deputy Chairman of the CLC in November 1985 and re-elected in November 1988, he held that position until October 1991. In November 1990 he was elected to the Alice Springs ATSIC Regional Council and was ATSIC Commissioner for the Central Australian Zone until 1993. He is General Manager of Tangentyere Council.

Tangentyere Council
Represents and provides services to the town camps of Alice Springs. The town camps were the subject of one of the first land

claims before Interim Land Commissioner Dick Ward. Although the claims were excluded under the final legislation the town camps were granted special purpose leases.

Tickner, Robert
Minister for Aboriginal Affairs since 4 April 1990. (He became Minister for Aboriginal and Torres Strait Islander Affairs on 19 December 1991).

Tilmouth, Bruce 'Tracker'
Director of the Central Land Council. Mr Tilmouth is a graduate in Natural Resource Management and was appointed Assistant Director in 1989. He became Director in February 1994.

Tiwi Land Council
Represents the traditional landowners of Bathurst and Melville Islands, north of Darwin. Originall part of the NLC region the separate Tiwi Land Council was established in 1978.

Toohey, John
Appointed as the first Aboriginal Land Commissioner in 1977 he served in that position until 1982. In 1983 he was appointed by the Minister for Aboriginal Affairs Clyde Holding to prepare a report on the Land Rights Act. He was appointed a Justice of the High Court of Australia in 1987.

Tuxworth, Ian
Chief Minister of the Northern Territory from 17 October 1984 to 14 May 1986.

United Nations Working Group on Indigenous Populations – WGIP
The WGIP is a subcommittee of the United Nations Human Rights Commission and has been meeting annually since 1983 to consider issues of indigenous rights and draft a Universal Declaration on the Rights of Indigenous Peoples. The CLC and other Aboriginal organisations have regularly sent delegations to participate in these sessions.

Vacant Crown Land
Land for which all interests are held by the Crown (see Alienated land) and which has not been dedicated for any public purpose.

Viner, Ian
Minister for Aboriginal Affairs 22 December 1975 to 5 December 1978.

Wentworth, William
Minister in charge of Aboriginal Affairs under the Prime Minister, 28 February 1968 to 31 May 1971.

Whitlam, Gough
Prime Minister of Australia 5 December 1972 to 11 November 1975. Minister for Aboriginal Affairs 5 December 1972 to 19 December 1972.

Wilson, Ian
Minister for Aboriginal Affairs 7 May 1982 to 11 March 1983.

Index

AAPA see Aboriginal Areas Protection Authority
Abbott, Barry, 102, 114
Aboriginal and Torres Strait Islander Heritage Protection Act, 40, 46, 60, 90, 107–109, 126
Aboriginal and Torres Strait Islanders Commission (ATSIC), 6, 68, 79, 85, 90, 96, 100, 102, 107, 120, 123, 125–128
Aboriginal Areas Protection Authority (AAPA), 80, 87, 90–91, 97–99, 102, 107, 126, 128
Aboriginal Land Fund Commission, 5, 9, 17
Aboriginal Land Rights (Northern Territory) Act 1976, 1, 8, 12, 15–17, 20–22, 24–26, 28–30, 34, 38–39, 43–44, 52, 56–59, 61, 64, 68–69, 72, 77, 79–80, 82, 84–85, 92, 94–97, 99, 113, 115, 121–129
Aboriginal Tent Embassy, 3
Aboriginals Benefit Trust Account, 53, 126, 128
Aileron, 66
Albrecht, Paul, 12
Alekarenge (Ali Curung), 14, 21, 30–31, 34, 75, 109–110
Alice Springs, 7–11, 17, 20–21, 23, 25–28, 30–32, 34–36, 38, 40, 43, 45, 47–49, 51, 53, 56, 62, 64, 66, 69–71, 78, 80–83, 87, 89–90, 94, 96–98, 100, 104, 109, 120, 123, 128
Alyawarr, 32, 40, 67, 98, 110, 115
Amoonguna, 7, 11–13, 20
Anderson, Alison, 112
Anindilyakwa Land Council, 100, 126
Anmatyerre, 77, 110
Areyonga, 66
Arrernte, 11, 41, 44–45, 67, 82–83, 85, 91, 102, 105, 109–110, 116, 125, 128
ATSIC see Aboriginal and Torres Strait Islander Commission
Atula, 76, 114

Australian Mining Industry Council (AMIC), 9, 39, 57, 126
Ayers Rock see Uluru
Barrow Creek, 61, 71, 75, 88
Barunga Statement, 72–73, 105–106, 110, 113
Baume, Peter, 29
Breaden, Kunmanara, 6, 25, 40, 55, 111, 113, 124–126
Brunette Downs, 1
Bulla, Peter, 105
Burke, Brian, 49
Burslem, Trevor, 104
Cabbage Gum Bore, 113, 120
Canteen Creek, 92
Carmody, Kev, 103
Cattlemen's Association, 44, 49, 66, 85, 89, 107
CCNT see Conservation Commission of the Northern Territory
Central Australian Aboriginal Congress, 38, 55, 58, 104, 128
Central Australian Aboriginal Investment Corporation, 116
Central Australian Aboriginal Legal Aid Service (CAALAS), 7, 9
Centrecorp Aboriginal Investment Corporation, 55, 60, 63, 95, 104–105
Chilla Well, 22, 89
Churches, 65, 69, 74
CLP see Country–Liberal Party
Clyne, Ben, 6
Coniston Massacre, 22, 31
Conservation Commission of the Northern Territory (CCNT), 45, 88, 96
Coombs, Dr HC 'Nugget', 8, 40–42
Coulter, Barry, 27, 60
Council for Aboriginal Reconciliation, 62, 93, 98–100, 106, 110, 127–128
Country Liberal Party (CLP), 13, 17, 48, 89, 127
Cowan, Zelman, 20
Cubadgee, 100–101

130

Daguragu, 1–2, 7, 10, 21, 34, 59, 87, 102–103
Department of Aboriginal Affairs, 4–7, 9, 22, 26, 32, 37, 44–45, 49, 56, 66, 69, 79, 123, 126–128
Devils Pebbles see Kunjarra
Djerrkura, Gatjil, 104
Docker River see Kaltukatjara
Dodson, Patrick, 41, 54, 57, 127
Doolan, Brownie, 105
Eames, Geoff, 9, 12
Ernabella, 10, 34
Evans, Gareth, 65
Everingham, Paul, 17, 26–29, 34, 38, 42, 127
excisions, 8, 13, 26, 29, 32, 41, 44–45, 49, 51, 53, 55, 57, 66, 69, 75, 82–86, 89, 99, 111, 116
Federal Council for the Advancement of Aborigines and Torres Strait Islanders (FCAATSI), 3
Federation of Ethnic Community Councils, 65
Finke, 105
Finke River Mission, 12, 127
Foley, Gary, 70
Frank, Jimmy, 101
Frank, Patrice Napurrurla, 78
Fraser, Malcom, 10, 17, 58
Furber, Rosie, 35, 81
Gorey, John, 45
Gray, Peter, 102
Gurindji, 1–4, 7, 21, 59, 67, 102–104, 115
Haasts Bluff, 14, 17, 20
Hamilton Downs, 26, 40–41, 114
Hand, Gerry, 66, 68–69, 77, 89, 127
Hardy, Frank, 2, 102–103
Hatton, Steve, 27, 71, 105, 116, 127
Hawke, Bob, 38, 42, 46, 49, 54, 56, 58, 66, 70, 72–73, 105–106, 117
Hay, David, 13
Hayden, Bill, 114
Health, 2, 115

Heaslip, Grant, 55
Hermannsburg, 14, 63, 76, 94, 111, 119, 127
Holding, Clyde, 27, 38–40, 46, 53, 55–56, 59–60, 65–66, 127, 129
Hollows, Fred, 2–3
Honeymoon Bore, 98
Intjartnama, 98, 110
Iwuputaka (Jay Creek), 14
Jakamarra, Frank Nelson, 113
Jampijinpa, Billy Bunter, 1
Japanangka, Dennis Williams, 73
Japanangka, Frankie, 77
Jay Creek see Iwuputaka
Johnson, Gregory, 37
Junction Waterhole, 87, 90–93, 97–99, 102, 107–109, 116
Junkurakurr, 118
Justice Woodward, 3–5, 7, 9, 12–13, 17, 126, 128
Kalkarindji, 8, 87
Kaltukatjara (Docker River), 108, 121
Kanari, Peter, 59
Kanttaji, 113, 120
Kanturrpa, 113, 120
Kaytetye, 31, 61, 71, 75, 88, 110
Kearney, William, 34, 38, 52, 54, 68, 127–128
Keating, Paul, 116–117, 119, 121–122
Kelly, Paul, 103
Kimberly Land Council, 120, 127
Kings Canyon see Wattarka
Kings Creek Station, 72, 85
Kintore see Walungurru
Kunapula, 121
Kunjarra (Devils Pebbles), 23, 75, 78, 89, 118
Kurundi, 115, 121
Lajamanu, 14, 20, 30, 92, 99, 103, 121
Lake Amadeus, 6, 28, 59, 72, 78, 85, 118–119, 122
Lake Mackay, 14, 20
Lake Nash, 26, 32, 38, 40
Land Claims
    Kanturrpa–Kanttaji, 113, 120

Lake Amadeus, 6, 28, 59, 72, 78, 85, 118–119, 122
McLaren Creek, 53, 75
Mistake Creek, 100
Mt Allan, 30, 71, 75–77
Mt Barkly, 28, 38, 54–55
Simpson Desert, 102, 105
Tanami Downs, 107
Ti-Tree, 30, 60, 109
Utopia, 17, 22, 24, 28
Warlpiri, 9, 17–18, 31, 77, 104
Warumungu, 19, 23, 28, 36, 40, 44, 51–52, 63–64, 74–75, 99, 115, 117, 120
Western Desert Land Claim, 104
Willowra, 19, 22, 24, 28, 38, 40
Yurrkuru (Brookes Soak), 99
Land Rights Act see Aboriginal Land Rights (Northern Territory) Act
Land Rights News, 11, 55, 70, 75, 85, 94
land management, 42
Lester, Yami, 29
Liberal Party, 3, 13, 17, 127
Lilla, 104
Lingiari, Vincent, 1–2, 7
Little Well, 37
living areas, 19, 26, 30, 39–41, 43–46, 49–50, 53, 69, 79, 82–84, 96, 116, 121
Long Pwerle, D., 75, 79, 84, 102, 109–110, 128
Loves Creek, 37, 114
Luritja, 6, 28, 67, 105, 109–111, 123, 126
Luther, Jupurrurla, 14
Lynch, Don 'Pop', 85
Lynch, Margie, 82
Mabo (Mabo v Queensland), 1, 111, 116, 119–122
Magellan Petroleum, 17, 20, 23, 26, 31, 92
Martin, Brian, 23–24, 60, 64, 80, 128
Mary Ann Dam, 118
Maurice, Michael, 49, 52, 60, 68, 128
McLaren Creek, 53–54, 75, 109, 115
Mereenie Basin, 17
Middleton Ponds, 6, 26

mining, 1, 4, 9, 11–13, 15, 20, 24, 29, 38–39, 45–46, 49, 51, 56–57, 59, 61, 64–66, 74–75, 78–79, 89, 92, 95, 99, 104–105, 109, 115, 121–124, 126
Mistake Creek, 100, 113–114
Morgan, Hugh, 45
Mpweringe–Arnapipe OutstationCouncil, 0, 26, 45–46, 49, 82–83, 86
Mt Allan, 22, 30, 71, 75, 77, 79
Mt Barkly, 28, 30, 38, 54–55
Mt Theo, 120
Murphy Jappanangka, 54, 115
Muṯitjulu, 8, 78, 95
National Aboriginal Conference, 51, 128
National Federation of Land Councils, 51, 93
Nelson Napurrula, Topsy, 89, 93, 102
Newcastle Waters, 1
Ngaanyatjarra, 30, 109, 116
Nixon, Peter, 3
North Flinder Mines (NFM), 95, 104
Northern Land Council, 4, 19, 23, 47, 49, 51, 55, 72, 75, 81, 100, 105–106, 110, 114, 120, 126, 128–129
Northern Territory Government, 6, 10, 13, 17–24, 26–31, 35–36, 38–44, 48–52, 55, 57–58, 60, 63, 65–66, 68–69, 71, 74–81, 83–85, 87–91, 93, 95–97, 99–100, 102, 105, 108–109, 112–115, 117–122, 124–125
Northern Territory Police Force, 3, 70, 89, 108
Nyininyi, 104
Nyirrpi, 92
Office of Aboriginal Affairs, 3
Olney, Howard, 71, 92, 128
One United Voice, 111
Ortmann, Max, 91, 102, 107
outstations, 8, 24, 37, 42, 45, 50, 55, 63, 117, 120–121
Palm Valley, 26, 36, 43, 60
Palmer, Agnes, 107
Palmer, Mike, 96
Papunya, 8, 24, 103, 108–109, 111–112

pastoralists, 1–2, 4, 6–10, 13, 15, 17, 19, 21, 23–24, 26, 28–30, 32, 37–40, 42–45, 49, 51–53, 55–57, 59, 65, 69, 75–76, 79, 83–84, 89, 96, 100, 105, 107, 109, 111, 114–116, 121–122, 128
Perkins, Charles, 9, 38, 44, 56, 128
Perron, Marshall, 35, 48, 80, 90, 93, 95, 97–98, 114, 116–117, 121, 125, 128
Petermann, 14, 20
Pilbara, 1
Pitjantjatjara Yankunytjatjara Ngaanyatjarra Council, 30
Plummer, Christine Napanangka, 78
Pope John Paul II, 62
Power and Water Authority (PAWA), 66, 78, 91–92, 102, 108–109, 111
Racial Discrimination Act, 121–122
Railway (Alice Springs to Darwin), 26, 47
Rangiari, Mick, 2, 103
referendum (1967 citizenship rights), 3
Regionalisation, 7–8, 51, 68, 78–79, 87, 96, 108, 114, 121, 126, 128
Ross, Kumantjayi, 82, 93–94, 102, 109–110, 113–114, 121, 124, 128
Rowland, Barry, 21, 25, 29, 128
Royal Commission into Aboriginal Deaths in Custody, 82, 97, 106, 127
Rubuntja, Wenten, 9–12, 16, 25, 35, 47, 57, 62, 67, 70, 72–73, 100, 119, 128
sacred objects, 10, 76, 84, 94, 107–108, 111, 113–114
sacred sites, 4, 10–11, 13–15, 17, 20, 23, 26–28, 31–32, 35–41, 45–47, 49, 52–53, 60, 64, 71, 75, 78–81, 84, 87, 89–91, 93, 95, 97–100, 102, 107, 109, 118, 121, 123, 126, 128
Sandover River, 98
Santa Teresa, 14, 20, 34
Scrutton, Stanley, 25, 40, 128
Seaman Inquiry, 38, 49
Shaw, Barbara, 88
Shaw, Geoff, 29, 57, 75, 95–96
Simpson Desert, 102, 105

Sons of Gwalia, 120
Standley Chasm, 74
Stephen, Ninian, 55, 58
stock routes and reserves, 30, 44, 49, 60, 65–66, 77, 83–86, 117
Strehlow Research Centre, 76, 84, 94, 100, 108, 114
Strehlow, Carl, 107–108
Strehlow, Kathleen, 111
Strehlow, T.G.H., 12, 94, 107, 111, 113–114
Stuart, Max, 100
Tanami Downs, 107
Tanami Joint Venture, 79, 95, 99, 102
Tangentyere Council, 38, 55, 104, 128
Tempe Downs, 6, 123
Tennant Creek, 8, 19–21, 23, 28, 34–35, 40, 50–52, 59–60, 63, 75, 78, 84, 99–101, 109, 113–114, 117–118, 125
Tennyson, Brian, 100
terra nullius, 1, 62, 111
Thangkenharenge, 71, 88
Ti-Tree, 30, 60, 109
Tickner, Robert, 90–92, 97–98, 100, 103, 105, 107–110, 117–119, 129
Tilmouth, Bruce 'Tracker', 113, 118, 123, 125, 129
Tiwi Land Council, 19, 51, 129
Tjamiwa, Tony, 57
Tnorula (Gosse Bluff), 41, 96
Toohey, John, 15, 24, 39, 129
town boundaries, 20, 52, 75, 117
treaty, 64, 66, 68, 72, 89, 93
Turner Jampijinpa, Lindsay, 73
Turner, Julie, 47
Turner, Silas, 49
Tuxworth, Ian, 28, 53, 57, 129
Ukaka, 104
Ulpanyali, 73, 104
Uluṟu, (Ayers Rock), 4, 6, 16, 29, 42, 45, 57–58, 67, 78, 114, 126
United Nations Working Group on Indigenous Populations, 74, 93, 102, 113, 129

133

Utopia, 17, 19, 22–24, 28, 34
Vale, Roger, 13, 48
Vincent, Victor, 103
Viner, Ian, 11, 13, 16–19, 21, 34, 129
Wakaya, 23
Walsh, Peter, 46
Walungurru, 24
Wanmara, 97, 104, 111
Ward, Dick, 128
Warlmanpa, 19, 21, 31, 33, 59
Warlpiri, 7, 9, 14, 17–18, 22, 31, 67, 69, 77, 102, 104, 109–110, 121, 123
Warumungu, 19, 23, 28, 36, 40, 44, 51–52, 63–64, 67, 74–75, 77, 99–101, 109–110, 115, 117–118, 120
Watarrka (Kings Canyon), 6, 63, 95, 97, 104–105, 111, 119
Wave Hill, 1, 7, 19, 103
Webb, Stephen, 90, 92–93
Werlatye Atherre, 27–28, 38, 71, 80–81, 90
Western Australia, 30–31, 38, 45, 49, 56, 82, 111, 127–128
Whitlam, Gough, 3–4, 9, 23, 102–103, 129
Williams, Ross, 117–118
Willowra, 5, 19, 22–24, 26, 28, 30, 38, 40, 75, 123
Wilson, Ian, 29, 129
women, 1, 28, 34, 47, 70, 73, 78, 81, 88–89, 93, 101, 103, 111, 116, 118
Woodward, Albert, 3–5, 7, 9, 12–13, 17, 126, 128
Wootten, Hal, 91, 108–109
Yambah, 26, 45–46, 49, 82–83, 86
Yankunytjatjara, 30, 109, 116
Yirrkala, 1
Yuelamu, 71, 75
Yuendumu, 13–14, 20, 22–23, 26, 30, 92, 108
Yulara, 50
Yunupingu, Galarrwuy, 51, 70, 72–73, 110
Yurrkuru (Brookes Soak), 99